LARRY LLOYD

HARD MAN:
HARD GAME

LARRY LLOYD

WITH RITA WRIGHT

HARD MAN: HARD GAME

JOHN BLAKE

Published by John Blake Publishing Ltd,
3 Bramber Court, 2 Bramber Road,
London W14 9PB, England

www.johnblakepublishing.co.uk

First published in paperback in 2009

ISBN: 978-1-84454-788-3

British Library Cataloguing-in-Publication Data:

A catalogue record for this book is available from the British Library.

Design by www.envydesign.co.uk

Printed in the UK by CPI Bookmarque, Croydon, CR0 4TD

1 3 5 7 9 10 8 6 4 2

Papers used by John Blake Publishing are natural, recyclable products made
from wood grown in sustainable forests. The manufacturing processes conform to
the environmental regulations of the country of origin.

Every reasonable effort has been made to contact the relevant copyright-holders. Any
omission is inadvertent; we would be grateful if the appropriate people could contact us.

To Dad, a man amongst men, and Mum, a grafter all her life; and the three rocks in my life: my daughter Yolanda, my son Damian and my granddaughter Georgia. Thanks for being there.

ACKNOWLEDGEMENTS

Bert Francis helped me realise that I could have future in football.

Bristol Rovers: Bill Dodgin, Bert Tann, Fred Ford – taught me how to be a professional and the importance of hard work.

Liverpool: Bill Shankly, Joe Fagan, Bob Paisley – took me from a boy to a man and instilled so much confidence in me with their faith in my ability.

The people of Liverpool: Sue and I moved to Liverpool as 20-year-olds, but the welcome we received from the Liverpool people made this enormous move so much easier.

Nottingham Forest: Brian Clough, Peter Taylor, Jimmy Gordon – after two uneventful years at Coventry, Forest signed me and gave me the second successful period of my football career.

The people of Nottingham: Having spent two years living in Coventry, the warmth of the Nottingham people was very welcome. My two children grew up in Nottingham and the four of us really enjoyed our time there.

Sir. Alf Ramsay: A gentleman. After the cup throwing, shouting style of management used by Shankly and Clough, Sir Alf introduced me to the cool, calm, calculating way of getting your message across. A welcome change.

Sue: Was with me from our school days and shared the good times and the bad. Her greatest gift to me was giving me two wonderful children, Yolanda and Damian, for which I can't thank her enough.

As a large part of my book is about the ups and downs of my personal life, I wanted a female ghost writer to assist me and to get her angle. In Rita Wright I found such a writer, and I thank her very much. Many thanks also to John Blake Publishing for having the insight to realise that I had a story to tell.

There are countless other people that I would like to thank, but to name a few: John Robertson, Sharyl, Sally, Les Bradd, Pat Millett, Fred, Ida, Sally and Mick Reacher, Bev, Charlie and Tracy, John Crofts, Alan Goodband, Paul, Graham, Kevin in Spain and many, many more.

CONTENTS

'As well as being a very, very tough player, he was terrific in the air and read the ball brilliantly. When I saw him flick the ball over Kevin Keegan's head when we were playing against Hamburg, and then, as cool as a cucumber, play it out to the wing, I knew we were going to win the European Cup. He was a star player when he was with Liverpool and he'd lost none of his hunger when he came to Nottingham Forest.'

John Robertson, 2008

LLOYD NO.5

SUMMER 2001

I am standing in the doorway of my bar in Spain watching the world go by at a snail's pace. They live by the 'Manyana Rule' on the Costa del Sol, which means everything gets done tomorrow, leaving you free to either siesta and enjoy the sunshine, or to fester with frustration if you are trying to get a job done and everyone else is taking a siesta.

Patience has never been my virtue, so I fall into the second bracket. I like to get stuck in and finish whatever needs doing. It has always been this way. So my empty bar is getting on my nerves. I wonder whether I might go for a walk down to the seafront and breathe in some fresh air, but decide against it because I am, after all, trying to run a business here.

Five o'clock hails Happy Hour and a few punters begin to drift through the door, so I smile a greeting and follow them back inside where I find the air conditioning has stopped working – something else to fix at that damned slow pace. Perhaps I can ask a Brit to fix it? And chance another rip-off! I don't think so. I love my fellow countrymen, but some of the undesirables who inhabit this neck of the woods beggar belief.

A burly man of Eastern European appearance is leaning on the bar. He is visibly struggling with the extreme summer heat and sweating profusely. The black suit he's wearing doesn't help. I ask him what he'd like to drink. 'Vodka?' I enquire, not really caring.

'Vladimir' leans annoyingly closer, invading my body space, and in a heavy accent asks, 'Do you have anything stronger?'

Hasn't he heard about the huge Spanish measures? Two Bacardi and cokes and you're on your back.

An elderly couple waiting patiently for their buy-one-get-one-free refreshments watch the interaction with boredom etched on their sun-baked faces, while the overhead fan refuses to whirr into life.

The dark and sinister Eastern European sniffs loudly to demonstrate his need to purchase drugs, so I show him the door. 'Fuck off, and don't come back', I growl. This is both very brave and incredibly stupid of me (two deeply ingrained traits of Lloydie's), as I am acutely aware that he is just as likely to pull out a gun and shoot me. Not because he's Eastern European, I might add – but simply because he's one of the *eclectic* ex-patriates who congregate on some areas of the otherwise beautiful Costa del Sol. If my body was found in a burned-out car, I would make front-page news in England, but it would only make a three-line story in the local paper, and then forgotten.

Thankfully, he turns and swaggers outside to seek cocaine elsewhere.

I throw a weak smile at the elderly couple. He's glowing from too much sun, and she is positively burned to a crisp.

'I thought we were in Spain,' says the wife. 'This place is just like being back in England. Bloody football – you can't even get away from it when you go on holiday.'

She is referring to the football memorabilia plastered all over the walls. Photographs, shirts, scarves – and they are all red and white. Where I once had a red and white house in Liverpool, now I have a red and white bar on the Costa del Sol.

As I open my mouth to offer a beer or sangria, the punter jumps in and cries out in a broad Northern accent, 'Hey! Didn't you used to be Larry Lloyd?'

I start to twitch. My nerves are not good at the moment.

'Who was Larry Lloyd?' asks the burned wife.

'He was a great footballer. Hey, those were the days when it was a real man's game. When the men got stuck in and had to play in all sorts of terrible weather conditions. Not like the mollycoddled wimps of today who get to play on heated pitches and are fed special pasta, protein and banana diets. They're not supposed to be fed on monkey's food. What's wrong with a plate of good old-fashioned pie and mash or a hot dog?'

The holidaymaker's got a point there.

He stands there rubbing his chin, remembering. I sense nostalgia.

I rub *my* chin in wonderment. Did I *used* to be Larry Lloyd? The last I knew it, I still was.

Turning to his wife, he begins to tell her all about this bloke called Larry Lloyd who he reckons used to be one of the best centre-halves to have ever played for the mighty Liverpool. 'You were one hard bastard,' he goes on.

Careful buddy, I still am hard-ish.

'Didn't he play for England too?' he asks, as if I'm not there.

'Yes, *I* did play for England on several occasions, and *I* captained the Under-23 team.'

'Didn't he play for Cloughie too?' the man asks me before he raises a beer to his lips and drinks thirstily.

'Yeah, at Nottingham Forest,' I say dryly.

'That's right, I remember everything now; he was in the newly formed Shankly team that lifted the UEFA Cup. I remember watching the team parading through the city of Liverpool, holding the trophy in the air.

'Ah! He was great in that No.5 shirt – looked good as well – the red suited him, what with his dark hair. Ah! I see now, that's why this place is called Lloyd No.5.

'Aye, he was a big lad. Some people called him a colossus; and others said he was like a brick wall. On a good day no one could get past him.'

I'm reminded just how much a football fanatic can go on... and on. They can talk for England about the game. At least *some* things never change. But clearly *I* have. Shit, I know I've lumped on the weight since I retired from football, but now I feel invisible.

Juan, a regular happy-hour drinker in my bar, arrives with his girlfriend Maria. He's a nice kid. I get him a cold beer.

Juan swigs from his bottle of San Miguel while drinking in the conversation and, more importantly, the atmosphere around him. He starts to ask about my football career as well.

I turn around and point to the huge signed photograph of me on the wall. I'm wearing a red football shirt and a wide grin. My arms are high in the air in celebration. 'That's me up there with the UEFA Cup. And the photograph next to it is me with the League Championship.'

Juan looks impressed. The Spanish love their football – are almost as fanatical as the British, if not even more so.

'Can I look closer?' asks Juan.

'Why not?' I think to myself. I stretch up and take down several photographs, including one of me that was taken in 1980. I am wearing another red shirt; only this time it's the Nottingham Forest kit. I am squatting down with my arms around the second European Cup I'd won with Forest — my third European triumph. I also choose another group photo to share with Juan.

Placing them on the bar in front of the young Spaniard, I watch his facial expressions. I'm not sure what I am wanting from this scenario. I think, if I'm honest, I want some validation of my life.

'Who are these other men?' asks Juan. 'Are they famous in England?'

He is too young to remember the men in the photograph. He's probably about the age of my son Damian, or perhaps he's Yolanda's age — somewhere in his mid-thirties.

We look at the pictures, and I identify the great players I have shared a pitch with — Tommy Smith, Emlyn Hughes, Kevin Keegan — and the great managers I have played under like Bill Shankly and Brian Clough. I recall the great matches, like the 1979 and 1980 European Cup finals I won with Nottingham Forest in our glory days. My best mate John Robertson scored the one and only goal at the Bernabeu Stadium in Madrid with his right foot, clinching our historic back-to-back triumph. What a night that was!

I can feel a tear prickling in the corner of my eye. I always get emotional when I talk about the good old days when I used to play top-flight football.

It's really weird, but the older I get, the more emotional I get. Everywhere I go everyone looks at me and sees this great big giant of a man and assumes I'm a total hard nut. I may have been a brick wall — a great big defensive centre-half who Bill Shankly reckoned would 'kick his granny for less than a fiver', but inside I'm mush.

The elderly couple finally stagger off. I'm pleased, it's people like them that make we want to pack the bar in. I had moved from

Nottingham to build a new life for myself, but it's not working. My second marriage is breaking down and I feel lost.

'I'm going to shut the bar, Juan,' I say. I walk across and pull the doors closed.

Juan is sharp enough not to ask why I am choosing to shut my bar just before it's due to get busy. 'Do you want me to go?'

'No, Juan, stay a while.'

I sit down on the stool next to him. He offers me a cigarette and then lights it for me. I take a drag, inhale deeply and then blow a smoke ring at the photograph of me and the other boys in red happily running around the pitch.

Juan has noticed I'm feeling lost. He's a nice guy, and I am glad of his friendship. True friends are hard to come by here. There are too many travellers drifting in and out of this corner of paradise to be able to forge deep friendships – but Juan is different.

I continue smoking my cigarette in silence, lost in a moment of nostalgia.

'Do you think football is better today, or was it better in your day?' he asks.

Now there is a loaded question that would take me forever to answer, and I tell Juan as much.

'I think we have time. Why don't you tell me about Larry Lloyd.'

I look at Juan's expectant expression, and I don't know where to begin. I wonder if I should start by telling him how fantastic football was a few decades ago. Dare I voice my opinion on how much I feel our great game has been destroyed by those in power today? How I believe the FA Premier League, the commercialisation of the game and influx of television revenue has ruined the working man's game?

No, perhaps that's a bit heavy to begin with.

LLOYD NO.5

'I don't quite know where to begin,' I confess. It was that lost feeling again.

'Why don't you begin at the beginning? Tell me about when you were a young boy, in the days before you became a legend.'

I make us some deliciously strong café cortado, and then pour two generous shots of brandy for the pair of us.

The atmosphere is now charged with expectation, and the sense of boredom that often fills my long days is replaced with an eagerness to recount my glory days in top-flight football.

Then a strange thing happens. Suddenly the dilapidated fan overhead whirrs into life, and we are fanned with cool air. It's an omen.

The scene is set – and so I begin… at the very beginning.

CHAPTER 1

LAURENCE VALENTINE LLOYD

BRISTOL 1940s/50s

I was born in Bristol on 6 October 1948, and it was my home for the first 20 years of my life.

Born into a large and warm family, I am lucky to be able to say I had a happy childhood. But it was different to most kids' home lives because my dad was blind. He was suddenly struck down blind in his youth. He said it was like someone just drew the curtains across the light, and he was plunged into darkness.

He met my mum at a club. Not a football club, but one where blind people could meet up with others who couldn't see. My mum wasn't blind, but she had spent all her life taking care of her blind parents.

Every Saturday night she would accompany her dad, Albert, to a lively social event in the centre of Bristol where she would be the eyes of the unseeing. This was her life, and one she enjoyed. For my mother, Rene, it was normal to communicate with these people

1

who, although they were disabled, led full lives and used their other acute senses to compensate for not being able to see.

It was during one of these Saturday-night social functions that she met my father, Tom, and, according to Mum, it was love at first sight for her.

She was only sweet sixteen at the time and, apparently, very innocent about the ways of the world. Thomas Lloyd, however, was much older. In fact, by the time he met Mum, he was 32 and had already been married and divorced.

At six feet two, he was a tall, dark, handsome man (I take after him), but Mum was five feet nothing – a petite, pretty young girl who, because of her circumstances, had lived a more sheltered life than other girls of her age.

If it was love at first sight for my mum, it must have been love at first touch for my dad, because it wasn't long before they were married and she was expecting the first of ten children.

My dad has always been my number-one hero. My adoration of him began before I was out of nappies and, although he passed away many years ago just as my career at Liverpool was taking off, I adore him still.

I must have been about five when my brother Ivan and I used to wait excitedly by the window for the first glimpse of our father returning from work.

Ivan was 18 months older than me, which set us apart from the rest of our siblings, as the age gap between most of us was three years. Because of this closeness in age, a firm bond was established between us – we were competitive but most of all we were mates and allies.

We would stick our heads under the front-room net curtains and watch and wait. When our dad finally turned the corner and appeared at the top of our road, we would boyishly shove each other out of the way and run as fast as our legs would carry us. I was always desperate to be the one who got to him first, and I guess this was when my competitive instinct was first born. If I wasn't the first to clasp his free hand – the other was holding a white stick – I would get the hump.

'Dad… Dad…' we would yell, drowning out the click, click of his metal stick on the pavement. As the gap between father and sons narrowed, we could see his smile widen until it was an ear-to-ear grin, and by the time we threw our arms around him he would be laughing out loud.

Although we were both desperate for that free hand, in the end it really never mattered who reached him first; just to be close and to be able hold on to part of him was enough.

Then, as we walked slowly home – eclipsed by this big broad man whom we adored – us boys would chatter on and on about everything and nothing.

When we got back to the house, Mum would always be standing there on the doorstep to greet us. Well, to welcome Dad really – she'd probably already had enough of our high jinx during the day.

Home was a humble house on a large council estate in Bristol. I lived there with Mum, Dad and six of my eight siblings. My eldest brother Barney and sister Marion had already flown the nest, but No. 40 Hottam Gardens was always full.

We had a man called Uncle Fred living with us as well. He wasn't a real 'blood' uncle but we kind of adopted him. Fred was of Indian origin; I think he came from Calcutta. Allegedly his real name was Eric – Eric the Indian… hmm. Anyway, as the story went, he lost his whole family in a house fire and only just managed to save himself from perishing by jumping from an upstairs window.

3

My mum and dad took pity on him and gave him lodgings for a few weeks while he recovered. That was way back in 1930s, but he never moved out – instead he became one of us, and was an integral part of our family until he passed away 40 years later. Good old Fred was a much-loved part of our family. What was one more mouth to feed?

Making ends meet was not easy. We still had ration books back then, so I'm sure the arrangement worked well both ways, as Fred's rent money would have come in very handy when my mum went shopping for food.

My father worked as a basket weaver, but this only brought in a limited amount of cash, so it was always a struggle to get by.

Mum took care of the housekeeping, as did many wives in those days, and she always did the best she could. I guess she was the chancellor of the Lloyd home.

Then there were all the babies she gave birth to – they needed constant around-the-clock care. I think it's difficult, if not downright impossible, for those of us who only have two-point-four children to comprehend what it must have been like to have ten kids. Actually, tragically one child died at birth. That must have been sad for my parents, but not uncommon. Some poor women lost lots of babies.

Mum died in her mid-seventies – pretty much a normal 'three score years and ten'. The doctor said she was totally worn out and more than ready for a rest.

I was a sensitive child and, as I was born soon after World War II ended, I have often wondered how much of an impact the war had on my parents and older siblings and, in turn, me.

Bristol had been unexpectedly bombed heavily and the Filton area, which is where some of my mother's family lived, was really badly hit. My mum told me the story about one of her brothers almost getting killed in a daytime raid that was totally unexpected. He had been playing around with some mates in the fields near to the Bristol Aero plane company (now Rolls-Royce), when the sound of the air-raid siren filled the air. They just kept on walking as they didn't know what else to do, but when they heard the distinct sound of the German planes they threw themselves to the ground. Peering up at the sky, they counted more than fifty enemy planes approaching.

Paralysed, they watched as the formation flew ominously close, and then suddenly it was total chaos as bombs were dropped all over the place. The noise, he said, was deafening and he was scared out of his mind.

Why they started to run, he couldn't say. Shock probably played a big part. But run they did – they ran for their lives. The only thing was, they ran towards the British Aero factory and slap bang into the centre of the chaos. Workers from the factory were frantically scrambling over a barbed-wire fence, cutting their hands to bits in the process.

My uncle said that they had looked so frightened, and that was when it hit home to them the seriousness of the situation.

They ended up throwing themselves head first into a small brick tunnel that had been built over a stream, and waited in terror for the raid to end.

When they emerged, they could see flames licking high into the sky. Smoke filled the air, as did the piercing sound of the sirens of the emergency services going about their business. But the worst was yet to come.

When my uncle reached the end of his road, he could see his house burning. It had had a direct hit and half of it was missing. Just imagine that! I had, many times, and it scared me half to death there might be another war. Jesus, we were terrified of those Germans. You know, living through the war must have filled people with such panic and fear. They never knew what was going to happen next.

Bristol was a target because of that bloody British Aero factory. In all, 91 workers were killed. Apparently, lots of skilled men were lost, especially toolmakers, which was another blow in itself.

The post-war days in the rubble of Bristol were tough, and it was into this stage of reparation that I was born.

I would not be exaggerating if I told you there were certain people and situations that terrified me as a child. I might have grown to become one of the toughest centre-halves England has ever known – even likened to greats like Jack Charlton – but as a kid I was quite a softie. Recurring nightmares scared me to death. Insecurity and anxiety were feelings that were never far away…

One day I came home from primary school to see the furniture of our neighbour, Mrs Dawson, strewn all over the street; the poor old dear was sobbing her heart out. My mum was attempting to pacify her, but not a chance – she was inconsolable. Even though I was no more than eight, I remember feeling *so* embarrassed for this older lady. So much so, in fact, that I snuck quietly past the spectacle, and through our front door, closing the drama firmly behind me. Quaking in my boots, I stood with my back to the door wondering what in hell was occurring that could cause our neighbour to cry so hard. It must, I decided, be all because of a terrible local bully called 'Shin-Tin', who I presumed must be a Chinese man. It must have been him who had thrown her valuables all up the street. But it was just my imagination running wild.

Oh, God! I prayed so hard he wouldn't come and terrorise us, too; after all, he'd tried plenty of times before. I knew this because I had heard him yelling through the letterbox.

LAURENCE VALENTINE LLOYD

My sister Marjorie, seeing me trembling by the front door, came to comfort me. 'What's up, Larry?' she said.

'It's that horrible Mr Shin-Tin. He's thrown Mrs Dawson's stuff all over the road. I think he's going to steal it. She's crying, Marj.'

Marjorie looked puzzled. 'Who? Who is stealing her stuff?'

'Mr Shin-Tin the China-Man.'

'Who on earth do you mean? There are no Chinese men living around here. It's the man from the council who has come to take her belongings away. She hasn't paid her rent, so she's being thrown out.'

Well, this didn't exactly dispel my fear. If he could be nasty enough to take *her* things, he could take ours as well.

'But he *must* be Chinese or Japanese because of his name... Shin-Tin!' I wailed. 'I've heard our Ivan calling his name out whenever he knocks on our front door. As soon as Ivan shouts out his name, Mum throws herself on the carpet underneath the window so he can't see her. At first I thought she had a bad back but then I realised she was hiding.'

My sister scratched her head for a moment before she burst out laughing.

I didn't like being laughed at – I even growled at that tender age. 'Don't laugh, Marj. It's not funny.'

When she finally calmed down she explained to me that Ivan hadn't been shouting at a man named Shin-Tin, but was calling a message out to the rent man 'she in't in'.

Ivan had been shouting through the letterbox at the bloody rent man, pretending she wasn't home, because we had no rent money.

I'd like to say this new understanding took my fear away, but it didn't. I remained terrified we'd be thrown out of our home. Every day as I came home from school I would hold my breath as I turned

7

the corner into our road; always expecting the worst. Relief would flood through me when all was well, and I could safely go indoors and find my tea on the table.

Tea on the table! What a joy! As were so many things I experienced in my childhood.

Every evening the tin tub was set in front of a roaring fire and we would all scramble to be the first in the hot clean water. If you were last in the bath, the water tended to be cool and murky. That said, murky or not, it was a warming experience.

Not so warm, however, was the trip to the outside toilet. It was bloody freezing in mid-winter. Most homes back then had outside lavatories – usually situated opposite the coal shed or bunker. In fact, if I think about it, going to the loo back in the forties and early fifties wasn't exactly a pleasant experience. There was no soft Andrex to wipe your bum on in the post-war days. We had to make do with old newspapers that had been cut into squares.

Mind you, it wasn't all bad, especially as we grew older. As well as the homemade squares, there were newspapers and magazines to read while contemplating the job at hand, and it wasn't too long before I was turning straight to the back page to read the sports news, before wiping my arse on it.

We might not have had many luxuries but we did have the television. It was tuned into BBC – the only channel available to most families. Later, though, ITV boomed from our screens, and I for one was pretty overwhelmed by the new varied programme schedules. If I'm honest, some of the adverts had a huge impact on my immature brain. Much later on, I was able to make a link between these images and some of the horrific nightmares I had.

I remember clearly the very first ad I saw on ITV – the 'Murray Mints… Murray Mints… too good to hurry mints'. That one was fun. But another one had me running for shelter behind the sofa. It was the Kleenex tissues advert.

Anyone who remembers this fifties ad will be wondering what the hell I'm on about, as it wasn't supposed to instil fear in the viewer, but, hell, I fled in terror as the box of tissues whirred towards the front of the TV set. It was coming at me, of that I was convinced! And that fear of something coming at me was to stay with me all my life, through a childhood where I would have night terrors of objects encroaching on my personal space, ensuring I'd wake up drenched in sweat, and in a right old panic.

As I grew older I'd scream to myself in my sleep, 'Wake up, you bastard! Wake up! Wake up!' And, when I *did* finally wake, my breath would be short, sharp rasps as I gasped for air. It was just horrible.

I wonder if one of the reasons I became a great defender – and, according to Brian Clough, the best attacker of the ball he'd ever seen – was because I needed to really go hard at whatever was coming at me. Perhaps it was a survival instinct.

Come to think of it, I have always hated crowds. I will never walk along in a group – always a few metres in front or behind. I wonder now if this fear stems from the advert or whether there has always been a demon inside that drives me to feel this way. Who knows!

What I do know, though, is it's lucky for me I was good enough to be playing on the spacious pitches rather than being a fan squashed on the packed terraces. I just know I couldn't have handled any of those packed surges that regularly occurred in the crowds.

Taking all this into consideration, just imagine my horror when, many years later, I witnessed first hand the Hillsborough disaster – a terrible tragedy in the world of football, and one I will speak of later in this book.

But back to the 'good old days of my childhood' – can you believe my mother gave me the middle name of *Valentine*! Oh, I took some stick for that, I can tell you. Apparently, she had a crush on a radio presenter who was called 'Valentine', and she took it into her head that it was a wonderful name – for a boy. It's nearly as bad as the Johnnie Cash song 'A Boy Named Sue'.

But I have another theory as to why I was given such an effeminate middle name (thank fuck it wasn't my first name – pass the ball over here, Valentine, you big fat bastard). As I said, there was a three-year gap between each of my siblings, except for me and my brother Ivan who was just 18 months older than me. I know I could have been an accident, but I reckon my mum was so desperate for another little girl that she couldn't wait the full three years for another child. With hindsight, I actually think both scenarios are likely to be true.

One thing I know for sure is that my mum loved to dress me in girls' clothes. It wasn't uncommon for me to skip up the street in a dress and girlie shoes. Bizarre!

Anyway, this came to an abrupt halt one day when I was about four or five years old. My brother Ivan and I had been invited to a fancy dress party. We got ready and then trotted along to the house of the kid whose birthday it was.

Ivan went as a soldier, and received loads of compliments. I, on the other hand, was wearing my usual feminine attire and got no praise whatsoever. Everyone assumed I had just come as 'Laurence Valentine Lloyd', complete with flowery blouse.

That was it. Game over. The fat lady had sung her last song, and I was in trousers – albeit short ones. *Girlie Lloydie* had given up dressing up. Just as well; I'd look pretty daft nowadays at twenty-something stone. I would look like a cross between Les Dawson and *Little Britain*'s David Walliams. I guess you could say I had also been

10

in danger of being 'the only gay in the village'. That I didn't grow up with gender issues is nothing short of a miracle really.

But there were two reasons for me growing into a full-blooded male. The first of these had to do with my dad being my hero, and the other was my love affair with sport.

I'm really not exaggerating when I say that my dad has actually been my one and only hero. I know it might seem strange, given that I have been lucky enough to have had the likes of powerful masculine legends such as Bill Shankly and Brian Clough managing me. But Tom Lloyd, my blind but handsome warrior, was the first to show me the way.

One of the highlights of our summers was the annual cricket match between the students at the blind school and the workers at the Blind Workshop.

Believe it or not, my dad used to play cricket. Yep – I know. How do blind men manage to play cricket? I'll tell you. For starters, they needed a few props.

The bowler rolls a ball filled with milk-bottle tops towards the batsman. How does he know where the batsman is standing? Because the batsman is standing about 20 yards in front of a tea-chest –banging the bastard furiously! When the ball gets near the batsman, he takes a wild swing at it – and, believe it or not, the bat and ball quite often make contact. It was a marvel to watch, I can tell you.

Everyone would scream, 'RUN', and the batsman and his partner would set off, obviously towards each other. There would be lots of banging on tea chests to guide the runners home, but more often than not they would collide. I tell you, it was pretty harsh – blood was drawn on more than one occasion. But for the 'seeing' spectators it was a hilarious summer special!

Those childhood days could have gone on for ever and ever as far as I was concerned. But puberty was beckoning and I had to grow up. What a bastard!

MY HERO

Dad never went into great detail about his childhood, but I know for sure it was hard. Unlike me, he must have welcomed his teenage years, as they would have represented freedom.

He told us many stories, but it was all a bit sketchy. What we knew for certain though, was that he was an orphan, and he hated the bleak orphanage in London that was supposed to be 'home'. Don't forget, we are talking about the beginning of the 20th century – *Oliver Twist* days.

I don't know what happened to my paternal grandparents, as my dad never spoke about them. I've often wondered whether his mother died from one of the diseases of that time or if his father was killed in the Great War; perhaps Dad never knew either. Maybe it was all left to his imagination. Whatever, he was left alone in a scary world.

There was no such thing as adoption of children in those dark days. Adoption was strangely only available to the grown-ups. People who had been bereaved could go into court with a friend and be adopted into their family. That way the adoptee could inherit his new family's wealth when they died. Rather like we adopted Uncle Fred into our home, except there was not enough dosh in our home to be left to Fred – not after we'd all got our grubby hands on it!

The authorities back in Dad's day were a bit cautious about adopting kids into new families, probably because they feared the kids would be exploited. Like I said – it was all a bit *Oliver Twist*. So children without parents grew up in bleak orphanages. With money generally tight, it was expensive to house, clothe and feed kids like my dad, let alone educate and prepare them to go into the big wide world. And by all accounts, there were plenty of orphaned kids at that time.

Dad often repeated the exciting but dangerous story about him running away as soon as he got the chance. He said, 'After walking miles and miles in shoes that weren't exactly comfortable, a coalman stopped and asked me if I wanted a lift. He asked me where I was going, and I said, "I'm going wherever you're going!"'

Without a moment's hesitation, he jumped aboard the filthy coal truck and thus began a long and tiring journey that took him from London to Stroud in Gloucestershire, and eventually Bristol.

It was during his youth that he lost his sight. According to him, he went blind after a serious case of sunstroke, which seems a bit odd to me. Whether this story is accurate I will never know, as he died when I was 21. I don't think his blindness could have been genetic as none of us kids ever had a problem – not with our sight anyway!

Bristol became Dad's newly adopted hometown and he met and married his first wife, but was divorced by the time he fell in love with my mum.

Tom Lloyd was an extraordinary man, and quite a character – with a warm and cheerful disposition. He was a fair bit older than my mother, but it was a true love affair from the beginning. There were some gasps when he and my mother took a shine to each other, and became inseparable. Mum might have been just sweet sixteen, but she knew what she wanted and she went for it.

My parents married before World War II, and had a long and successful marriage. Despite his handicap, Dad always remained upbeat and he kept our family together spiritually. I suppose you could say he had a special aura about him, rather like

13

the Ayrshire legend Bill Shankly, who was one day to become a mentor of mine.

I came to the conclusion early in life that people who are handicapped in some way are blessed with other qualities. In my dad's case, he had umpteen positive virtues, but the one that outshone the rest was his knack of being able to break down what seemed an insurmountable problem into something manageable. Maybe the childhood and teenage problems we had were minor compared to his upbringing. So sifting through our dilemmas and dramas was dead easy for him.

I became aware of his wonderful patience and ability to give sound advice during my teens, when he helped me mull over difficulties I was having at school, but it really began much earlier when I was a toddler when Ivan and I would snuggle up either side of him and listen to his wonderful – even though a tad crazy – bedtime stories.

The one I loved the best (and the one I heard the most!) was about a 'Milk Horse' called... wait for it... 'Dobbin the First'.

Dad's imagination knew no bounds. Dobbin, who began his life as a horse who used to pull the milk-cart around Bristol, had a thirst for fame, and nothing would deter him from reaching his goals. After failing and falling down time and time again he eventually realised his ambition and won the Grand National. Hmmm!

It was a funny and cute story for sure. But on another level it was also a wonderful subliminal message to give a young boy about following his dreams.

He called another story 'The Underworld'. This was a pretty scary tale, but it had a happy ending, so that made it all right! It was about Middle Earth, and looking back it was a *Lord of the Rings* type of story.

LAURENCE VALENTINE LLOYD

I don't know where he got these endless stories from. I know he used to read lots of books in Braille, but I am certain these stories were born out of his great imagination. But then I guess if you are brought up in a crowded orphanage with lots of other children with dreams of a better life you are bound to develop a colourful world of fantasy.

Dad would sit on either Ivan's, or my, bed for story-time, until the day came when the roles reversed and us boys sat on the end of his bed and listened to him dishing out advice about the meaning of life. We chatted about everything from girlfriend problems to talking over difficulties I was encountering at school, and then later on challenges in my early football career.

Before my father died, he suffered a long drawn-out illness that saw him shrink from a big colossus of a man to a shadow of his former self where the cancer had invaded his stomach making it impossible to absorb nourishment. As his health deteriorated and he became desperately sick, we had to move his bed downstairs. I am certain he spent much of his time waiting for our arrival home. He knew which of his brood was there by the way we put our key in the lock and closed the door behind us. Even more than that, he could identify our own individual way of walking down the hallway. He always called the right name cheerily, and we in turn would pop our head around the living-room door and say goodnight.

More often than not, I was the last home, and on many occasions I was not merely content to say goodnight and go to my room. Instead I would perch myself on the end of his bed, and we'd chat on and on about everything under the sun. Afterwards I always went off to bed feeling that I had no problems at all, and would fall into a sound sleep. He seemed to have all the answers and I loved him for that.

15

HARD MAN: HARD GAME

Without a shadow of a doubt, the biggest regret of my entire football career was my dad being unable to see me kick a football – not in my childhood, nor throughout my teens. Later he missed seeing me play for some of the best teams in the country. A staunch nationalist, he would have revelled in the vision of me playing in defence for England against Germany, but instead he used to glue his ear to the radio and tune into his vivid imagination. This may or may not have been good enough for him – but it was fucking terrible for me.

CHAPTER 2

SCHOOL DAYS

AS A TEN-YEAR-OLD attending Filton Avenue Junior School, the highlight of the week was representing my school playing football. I just loved the whole competitiveness of it, and still, today, can't get my head around those who believe competitive sport in school is wrong. Life is one big competition – we compete in everything we do, and the sooner we learn all about the joy of winning and the disappointment of losing, and how best to deal with these emotions, the better.

The pride I felt in being school captain at the age of ten was as strong as later on – a decade later to be exact – when Sir Alf Ramsey invited me to captain his Under-23 team. That ten-year-old boy still resides deep inside me, and rises up in childlike wonderment when amazing things happen.

At Filton Avenue, it was my job as captain to go around to several classrooms to inform the lads who had (and who hadn't) been selected to play football the following day. Some faces lit up while others looked miserable. It really was a big deal to get to play – or get left out!

We had this teacher called Mr McGrath – a right old bastard he was too, a real tyrant. After I had read out the names of those picked for the Saturday game, I would yell out, 'And don't forget to bring kit with you.'

McGrath always growled the same response: 'Not bloody likely!'

I found this behaviour very strange, not to mention rude. I used to shake my head and mutter a few expletives under my breath, but would never have dared to challenge anybody in authority. That was all to change later, but as a mere pubescent I found his attitude unnerving.

Then another teacher enlightened me. 'Larry, did you know that McGrath has a daughter called "Kit"?'

After splitting my sides with laughter, I digested this information. So, every Friday night at team-naming time, I had great fun emphasising the word 'Kit', while watching McGrath's face twist with anger. I played on his weakness, basically – a skill that was to help me when, as a man, I pulled on the No.5 shirt.

I took and passed my Eleven Plus at Filton Avenue, and therefore slipped into the grammar stream at Lockleaze Comprehensive School. Unfortunately, my academic prowess went downhill fast when I discovered the wonderful world of sport.

It was football, basketball, cricket and rugby all the way. Sport, sport and even more sport – the obsession had set in, and I loved it all with a passion. It was fortunate for me that the school put lots of emphasis on sport, but there was a downside. Mr Allen – Head of Sport – was a rugby nut, and was therefore a devil for putting rugby on a higher pedestal then football. Outrageous crime!

This meant we had to play rugby every Saturday morning before going off to play football for either Manor Farm Boys or Westbury Whirlwinds in the afternoon.

Then a wonderful thing happened. Along came another teacher, Mr Brown, who was football crazy. Oh, what a great day it was when it was announced we could share the winter/spring terms between ruggers and footie! Rugby up till Christmas, and football after the seasonal festivities – that was, until the cricket began in the summer term.

It was also a great tradition for our school to play superb basketball. I am certain that, had I not pursued a football career, I would have enjoyed some success as a basketball player.

I was tall and strong and lucky enough to possess every attribute needed to make a good footballer.

I had an eye for a ball, and could therefore put my skills into play in most sports. I'm sure this is the case for many great sportsmen – you've either got it or you haven't and if you've got it and work at it you will eventually make the grade.

I continued playing football for the local teams. One of my team pals, an awesome guy called Richard Hook was also damned good. I think I can safely say that, had basketball been a professional team game in this country then, we could easily have made a good living from the game. But that was not to be his course, and certainly not mine. Even though I loved basketball, I knew in my heart my future lay in professional football.

I was appointed school games captain. This was a great honour and one I cherished dearly. But being a great 'all rounder' began to bring a whole set of problems for me. Fixtures were forever clashing and tricky choices had to be made. My personal decision was never difficult though; as far as I was concerned, football came first – end of.

The law of averages told me that one day there would be an incredibly important choice to be made – and that day came when I was 15.

I had a passion that was burning inside me, and this was the force I needed to help me make it to the top of my profession – but at times that passion was also the enemy. Sometimes I could be so hot-headed, and then I'd let rip without thinking things through properly.

What happened when I was 15, and how I reacted, was to bring about the first of many learning curves for me. There would be more to come later, under the management of Shankly, Clough and Sir Alf Ramsey. But for now I had to cope with the dilemma presented by my normally mild-mannered headmaster, Mr Langley.

I had been chosen to play football for Bristol Boys in an English Schools Trophy fixture against Mid-Somerset Boys. On the same day, I was selected to represent England Schoolboys at basketball. We were set to play West Germany at Loughborough. Of course I felt proud, but...

When I informed Langley that I was actually playing football for Bristol Boys that day, he went uncharacteristically ape-shit. 'But this is a much more important game!!!!' He was yelling his head off. 'A *much* bigger occasion – this is a chance for a Lockleaze boy to play for his country, and you say you've got to play for a local football team. Are you mad, Lloyd? Think of all the prestige it will bring to our school. We have never had an international sportsman here before. I insist you play basketball.'

Up jumped the new fierce Lloydie – the lion who was one day going to roar his way to European and domestic triumph. 'I am playing football for Bristol Boys. I promised them, and my word is as good as my promise. Sorry.'

Huh! I was sorry all right. I certainly paid for being stubborn and standing my ground for my beliefs.

'If you don't play basketball for England, I am going to strip you of your position as school football captain.'

My chin nearly hit the fucking floor. I couldn't believe what I was hearing. But there was worse to come.

'And what's more, you will not be allowed to play for the school in any sport. I will ban you from going anywhere near the gym or sports fields.'

This was blackmail – surely?

I could feel the tears welling up inside me. I felt crushed, furious and bewildered all at the same time. The conflicting emotions were too hard to bear. The bastard had got me by the balls. How could I back down? How could I go to the Bristol Boys and say, 'Sorry, lads, you're not as important as me going off to play a basketball glory game.'

I wasn't going to do it. I would *not* back down from my firm belief in loyalty to a football team.

The following months were the darkest I'd ever known and, looking back, I realise I fell into a deep depression – a depression that has visited me on more than one occasion during my life. I felt lost. I *was* lost. I am not exaggerating when I say that I felt as if a chunk of my heart had been ripped from me and nothing seemed to matter any more. I walked around in a permanent daze, which was most untimely, as my O Levels were rapidly approaching. Filled with frustration, I had nowhere to expel this vast energy, so it just whooshed around inside me.

I had always been academically capable, but in this state of mind I found I couldn't concentrate and, drowning in a sea of despair, I became quite panicky. I was totally incapable of shaking off this spell

21

in the doldrums. Needless to say, I didn't fare well in my exams — exams in which it had been presumed I'd succeed.

My parents were disappointed and dismayed. I'd passed my Eleven Plus and therefore hopes for at least *some* good results had been high.

Failure to achieve any was blamed on my being too heavily involved in sport, but this was not the case, and I lived alone with the truth that my head had gone to mush when sport was stolen from me. Sport that had already become a central part of my identity — that defined who I was. I was proud to be a sportsman.

In defence of Lockleaze School, I have to say that my whole experience there was otherwise pretty good, and when the time came to leave I was sad. Passing my Eleven Plus and earning a place in a school where opportunities were in abundance, and sport high on the agenda, most definitely set me on a road to success. Not too many lads from my humble beginnings get such opportunities — especially today.

I had been well within my comfort zone in school, but now I was set to leave and make my way in the big wide world beyond. And what a big wide world it was!

It all began at Bristol Rovers FC. At the age of 14, I was the first ever associate schoolboy to sign for the club. I was on my way. The die had been cast!

CHAPTER 3

GET A PROPER JOB!

I WAS FOOTBALL crazy ever since I can remember – probably ever since I gave up wearing the 'girlie' clothes.

Any of you who are football mad will know what it's like to adore your local team. Usually there are two rival teams – so you pick your side and you give them undivided loyalty. Liverpool love Liverpool and absolutely detest Everton. Bill Shankly wouldn't even use the word 'Everton'; instead he used to refer to them as 'the blue lot across the park'!

Manchester United and Manchester City hate each other, as do Arsenal and Spurs, Nottingham Forest and Notts County... well, I could go on and on – but for me there was Bristol Rovers and Bristol City.

I had no hesitation about which team I was going to follow – and play for – it was Bristol Rovers. Maybe it was because they were the best team, and all kids want to support a team that does well. Later, if the team plays like shit, you can have a good old rant about it but still love them. But in the beginning when you are at school and all your mates ask, 'Who do you support?' you really want to be able to say the name of a team that's doing well – and the Rovers were definitely doing better than the City.

I already knew I was going to be a footballer. I didn't know to what level I'd get, but I was going to give it everything I'd got. When I was old enough I was going to play for Bristol Rovers.

They had been an established team since way back in 1883 when they were called Black Arabs FC, and then they changed their name to Eastville Rovers, then Bristol Eastville Rovers before they eventually decided on Bristol Rovers in 1898.

The club's official nickname has always been 'The Pirates' because of maritime history and they are also known as 'The Gas', because of the gasworks next to Eastville Stadium. Pirates and Gas – quite something!

I was desperate to be an apprentice footballer, but there was no way – lack of money put paid to that teenage dream. Instead, I had to go and get a proper job. Christ! How many of us have heard that old chestnut? *Get a proper job with a proper wage and be sensible – everyone would love to be a sportsman, artist, actor, singer… and so on… and on!*

Of course, when you become a parent yourself, you begin to see the sense of this boring attitude, but when you're an ambitious teenager it sucks.

I signed an apprenticeship with a construction company called Modern Engineering. No offence to the company, but fuck, it was horrible. I hated every goddamn moment I was there – but, in all honesty, I was rarely happy when I was off the football pitch.

I persevered at Modern Engineering for 18 long months before I began to see a bright light ahead of me. I had no choice.

My day consisted of going across town to work, back across town for my tea, and then I'd dash over to Eastville – the home of Bristol Rovers – where I trained religiously and endlessly. With the

24

professional coaching I received there I moved rapidly through the junior teams; I was the only boy sweating his bollocks off with a poxy 'day job'. It was a bit of a bummer, I can tell you. You could say I was a teenager with a serious hump. Feeling sorry for yourself is not exactly an attractive trait – but it's also not an easy one to give up until you actually begin to realise that life in general is not fair.

Very occasionally I would take a 'sicky' from work so that I could train during the day with the real pros. But I chose my days carefully. I would only risk it when Bill Dodgin, the assistant manager at Rovers, would be there – as he always gave me lots of one-to-one coaching.

Bill was such a great guy, and luckily he recognised the potential in me, both in my playing ability and attitude. He took me under his wing, and during rest periods in training he never stopped talking to me about players he'd coached when he was a manager at clubs such as Southampton and Sampdoria in Italy. He had also managed Fulham in the late forties and early fifties – a club there would one day be some speculation about me joining. This was a pivotal moment in my budding career. So fascinated was I by his great stories I became even more determined to make it to the top of my profession. I *was* going to be a professional footballer – and that was that.

My skills improved no end under the watchful eye of Bill Dodgin – in fact, my game in general was getting better and better, and so it should have come as no surprise that scouts began to sit up and take notice of me.

Scouts and selectors were of major importance back in the sixties. If you were a young lad from a humble background kicking a ball about on a pitch in, say, somewhere like Scunthorpe, you had a chance of being discovered. Unlike today. Today we have the era of the agent, where, if you aren't already in a youth team, you need a miracle to get spotted.

Anyway, one particular scout was a representative of the England Youth Team. He put the word around about me and the next thing I knew I had been invited to go to Wolverhampton where they were holding trials.

Oh boy, I was as nervous as hell. My legs were like bloody jelly. But somehow I managed to conquer those juvenile nerves and, I tell you, I played my socks off. But I was confused about how good or bad my performance had been. I just couldn't judge how I'd played. I *thought* I'd had a good game – but I didn't really have a clue what they thought of me and my abilities.

As it turned out, those first trials had been good enough, and I didn't have to wait too long to find out. A letter dropped through our letterbox (much more welcome than a visit from Shin-Tin!), and it was for me. It told me, 'You have been invited to travel to Aberdeen to represent England against Scotland.'

Oh, fuck! My birthdays and Christmases had arrived all at once. I had earned a cap for England. Now my appetite for the game had reached fever pitch.

I have already hinted about the differences in football in the sixties compared to the game today, but communication wasn't at its best back then, and I found this out first hand. The football world is a very different ball game today!

Imagine this scenario happening in the 21st century.

There I was, on my way home from a hard day's work at the factory, sitting on the top deck of a bus in the centre of Bristol, when I noticed a copy of the *Bristol Evening Post* lying on the seat next to me. I picked it up and, like most sports fans, I went straight to the back page. There in bold print were the words: 'Larry Lloyd Plays in Tonight's Gloucestershire Cup Final'.

My mind was all over the place. I felt as if I had been hit by a sledgehammer. Stunned, shocked, bewildered, I read it all over again. How could this be possible? I didn't know a damn thing about this. Yes, there was excitement flooding my veins and, yes, I felt an adrenalin rush of anticipation, but, heck, this was unprecedented. No amateur had ever, *ever*, played in this important derby between Bristol Rovers and Bristol City, where players would lay down their lives to be given the chance to fight for local victory. Both clubs *always* picked their strongest team. These matches were hard-fought, aggressive affairs, with huge crowds cheering and jeering.

With these conflicting emotions threatening to overwhelm me, I jumped from the bus and raced all the way home, where I showered, collected my kit and then raced over to Eastville.

I swear, I had never moved so fast in my life, and the chatter going on in my head was beginning to get on my nerves. It wouldn't stop.

Why in God's name hadn't anyone bothered to tell me I'd been selected? How on earth was it that I got to know about it by reading it in a copy of the local paper? What if that copy hadn't been sitting there on the seat next to me? If I'd known I had been picked, I'd have thrown a sicky. Instead, I'd be the only player on either side to have been humping great lengths of steel around all day, instead of resting and physically and mentally preparing. Shit – life can be a bitch.

I couldn't answer any of these questions that were rattling around in my head. Had I not listened properly? Had I missed this important information? Perhaps my mind was racing so fast and so full of dreams and ambitions that I forgot to actually listen to people?

But it didn't take long to get my football head on and think positively. I was playing and that was all that mattered. These tough physical games had never fazed me. What did bother me, however, was the brilliant centre-forward I was up against – Hugh McIlmoyle, an experienced City player. I feared the opposition might be tough, and they were. They beat us 3–1, and I was gutted. Defeat of any kind gave me the hump, always did, always will. I'm a bad loser. I think most people who make it to the top of their profession are bad losers.

Back in the dressing room, I showered and licked my wounds – as we all did. Then something happened that lifted my spirits – someone had crumpled up a ten-pound note and shoved it inside my shoe. As an apprentice, I only earned five pounds a week, so you can imagine how much this meant to me. It was a hell of a lot of money. I knew that it was totally illegal for an amateur to be given a wage, and so it was no surprise that nobody owned up to this generous gesture, but I feel certain my mentor Bill Dodgin was behind it. Cheers, Bill!

Then I was brought down to earth with a bump. Manager Bert Tann began to stroll around the dressing room, chatting about the game, and generally trying to make us feel better. I was in awe of Bert Tann, and as a young player I hung on his every word. He loved Bristol Rovers with a passion, and had a 'no sell, no buy' philosophy. He wanted players at the club long term.

Then he announced, 'Despite our defeat here tonight, I am going to give you all the day off tomorrow.'

I could almost hear my early-morning alarm bell ringing in my ear right there and then. There was something very wrong going on – and I was going to sort it. I decided I was beginning to understand the saying 'What doesn't kill you makes you stronger'.

So, the following morning I leaped out of bed at seven, took the bus across town to work and did my obligatory time in the factory.

I *would* be a professional footballer, I damn well would. And as I humped heavy steel around for nine hours I channelled my rage into a fierce determination that it wouldn't be long now. I'd be a pro soon!

CHAPTER 4

I WILL BE A PRO!

I WAS A TEENAGER on a mission and no one was going to get in my way. My aggressive behaviour and tenaciousness has both helped and hindered my career. It has ensured tremendous success, but has also got me into hot water. This is part of the fabric of who I am.

My first encounter with the football disciplinary authority came during the 1966–67 season when I was playing regularly as an amateur in the Bristol Rovers reserve team.

It was a Friday night – the night before we were scheduled to play against Oxford United reserves at Eastville. I was having a great night over at my girlfriend Sue's house, and it turned into rather a late one.

It was unusual for me to have a booze the night before a match – in fact, I think this turned out to be both the first and the last for a very long time.

The next day I was tired and sluggish, and not the way a defender should feel, especially when marking a player called Colin

Harrington who had the reputation of moving so fast he could catch pigeons!

I was all over the place and, needless to say, I mistimed a tackle which saw poor old Harrington writhing on the floor in agony.

Foolishly, I had stood on his chest, and without a moment's hesitation the referee dismissed me. He could do nothing else. I had been out of order. Larry Lloyd had received the first of many red cards.

I was so mad at myself for being such an idiot and not preparing properly. This stupidity had set in motion a string of mistakes. Sleep deprivation, a body full of chemicals and a monster headache put me at a dreadful disadvantage. I should have been stamping on myself, not Harrington.

Others stamped on me though! Fucking hell, did I ever get a roasting. Bobby Campbell, the reserve-team coach, ripped my head off. Phew, it was unbelievable. But the worst was still to come.

Ten days later, I received a letter from the FA informing me I had been fined ten pounds. A hefty ten pounds lost in one swoop – two weeks' money at Modern Engineering. In effect, I'd lost the secret bonus someone had left in my shoe. What a doughnut I'd been.

I naively thought Bristol Rovers would pay the fine but sadly this was not the case. Forking out myself meant being unable to pay my board, which seriously pissed off my mum; and Sue was none too happy either, as I couldn't afford to take her out for ages.

I had upset everyone that I cared about, but I really had learned a valuable lesson. I would be sent off many times during my long career, but never again did I walk out on to a pitch unprepared.

Lots of great things happened during my spell as an amateur. As well as playing regularly for Bristol Rovers reserves, I also represented Gloucestershire Youth and England Youth. In fact, in one of these games I found myself up against a boy from the Liverpool area who would one day be both my enemy and friend – one Joe Royle – but there was no way back then we could have known that we would play against each other on either side of Goodison Park.

By the end of the season, my frustration at not being able to turn professional because of my financial situation had come to boiling point. I went to my parents time and time again to see if they had softened about my giving up my day job to pursue my career in football. But they said I had to keep my feet on the ground and earn a living. I also knew how much my wages helped out at home.

I know jealousy is a terribly unattractive emotion. It is also dangerous and can be destructive. They don't call it 'the root of all evil' for nothing. I used to get so envious when I heard my fellow players talking about their extended two-month holidays. Grrrrr... What did I have to look forward to? A boiling-hot summer of long days sweating my bollocks off in a stifling factory – and all for a fiver a week. A proper job, my arse. Yeah, yeah, I know, I was investing in my future and working towards independence and ensuring I'd always be employed, but – and this is a BIG but – I didn't want to be a fucking steel worker. This strapping great big ball of testosterone with a burning ambition WANTED TO BE A GODDAMN FOOTBALLER!

Little did I know that, while I was silently fuming away about my amateur status, there were clubs falling over themselves to sign me. All of this was kept from me and, until this day, I'm not really certain why. I would like to think that the club were nurturing me and biding their time until they felt I was both physically and mentally ready for the next step of my footballing career.

Just as I hadn't known about being included in the team to play the Gloucester Cup final match, so I was kept in the dark about the likes of Bristol City, Swindon Town, Southampton and Portsmouth all wanting to sign me. I would like to think they were taking care of me as I grew into a character who could cope with the tremendous strains of life in the fast lane. I would like to think they were pacing me, and waiting for the right time to sign me up.

As for me, the only team I had ever visualised playing for was the team I had watched from the terraces since I was eight years old.

Being told to go and get myself an apprenticeship in a proper job had been the first great disappointment of my career. Being a constructional engineer was not my idea of fun, as it was a grandiose name for a navvy who humps steel around. I wanted a contract with Bristol Rovers – that was that.

I had no idea for a very long time that Bert Tann was a great friend of Bill Shankly's. That said, even if I had, I would never have dreamed in a million years that I would be off to Anfield. Instead, I would sit for hours on end wondering how I could make things happen for myself. Bert Tann may have had an abundance of patience, but I needed instant gratification.

What could I do? I had to be proactive. Well, there seemed only one thing I *could* do, and that was to take the bull by the horns and force some changes. I knew I was good enough, and that knowledge was enough to spur me on to make an appointment to see Bert Tann.

It was May 1967, and my life was about to change forever. As luck would have it, my sister (who had set me straight about the Shin-Tin misunderstanding), now married and called Marjorie Hall, had been working her way up in the administration department at Bristol Rovers, and had landed a job as Bert Tann's secretary.

Marjorie was one of the first women to hold such a lofty position in what had always been a male-dominated world. Nowadays, we see many women involved in the sport, but back in the sixties it was practically unheard of.

So it was with Marjorie that I made my appointment to see the manager.

I marched in with my head held high, determined I was going to walk out a professional. I opened my mouth to speak, but Bert Tann was one step ahead of me. 'Tell me, Larry, do you think you are good enough to be a professional footballer?'

His direct approach knocked me off balance a little. For a while I just stood there gawping, unsure in my confusion how to respond. Then our eyes met. It was a powerful moment and one I'll never forget. Eventually I found my voice – one that was unrecognisable and sounded as if it had come out of the depths of my bowels. 'Yes, I think I am.'

Silence hung in the air for what seemed like an eternity, but in reality it could only have been a matter of seconds before he smiled and said, 'OK, Larry, I'll give you a twenty-five-pound signing fee, and a two-year contract at seven pounds a week.'

I gasped, opened my mouth, and then shut it again. He hadn't finished talking.

'Only on the condition your parents agree. So I suggest you go home and call a family meeting. I don't want to rock any boats. Come back tomorrow and let me know what it's to be.'

I emerged in a daze to see Marjorie sitting behind her desk wearing a wide grin. I knew in an instant that she knew Bert was going to offer me a contract. 'You rotten sod, why didn't you tell me?'

Shrugging, she told me she'd been sworn to secrecy. Bert had wanted to be in a position of power when negotiating money.

I was a bit pissed off at that, but so happy that I forgave her. Anyway, when we got back home, 'our Marj' was totally in my camp when trying to persuade Mum and Dad to let me give professional football a shot.

The message that was coming across to me loud and clear was how much they were impressed with my ability to play at a high level, but even more than this was my tenacity and sheer determination.

I was on cloud nine and thought I'd never come down, and then Marj told me, 'Mr Tann has been keen for you to turn professional for some time, but he wanted to see how long it would take you to muster up the courage to approach him.'

How about that! He was testing my courage. What a load of bollocks – he was just saving himself a few bob by being in the driver's seat when it came to the matter of my wages!

This was my first lesson in the politics of contract signing and wages – but it wouldn't be the last. If I thought Bert Tann was a crafty old goat, I was yet to have dealings with Bill Shankly.

When I eventually signed as a professional, Tann made me stay on for extra training, and he made me carry on with the amateur training nights on Tuesdays and Thursdays. I used to hate the old bastard. There were many occasions I could have punched him through the wall – and I'm sure he felt the same. Yet now I can look back and appreciate what a good job he'd done in ensuring I became the very best I could be.

CHAPTER 5

GOAL!

IN MID-JULY 1967, I reported, along with the other professionals, for pre-season training, and, despite everyone telling me how hard the next four weeks preparing for a season in the Third Division would be, I thoroughly enjoyed the whole experience.

I was a local teenage boy playing for the team he had adored since the age of eight, and who had completed the first leg of accomplishing his dream – to be the best centre-half in the land.

I was wearing the No.5 shirt and totally at ease. I had found myself, and was on my way to becoming a legend. But for now I had to be content with running around the pitch with a bunch of players who were *my* heroes.

As a kid I had queued for hours to get autographs from the likes of Ray Mabbutt (father of Spurs player Gary Mabbutt), Alfie Biggs, who was an absolute icon in Bristol, the uncompromising full-back Dougie Hilliard, not to mention Gloucestershire cricketer and tricky right-winger Harold Jarman.

Wow! How could my life possibly get any better? But it did. This was my new life and my new identity – Larry Lloyd, professional footballer.

Playing at centre-half, you rarely get a chance to score a goal, as you are usually defending more than attacking. I had never ever scored before. But one day I scored, and the feeling was unbelievable. If I *could* describe it, I would have to yell all about it from the rooftops so that everyone could share my euphoria. 'It's exhilarating – it's a buzz... it's...' Nope, there are no words brilliant enough to describe it. That must be why we all kiss and hug each other, punch the air or slide across the pitch while banging our chests like gorillas. Whenever I watch such spectacles on the television, I fill up with emotion, and remember my first goal.

We were playing Mansfield Town reserves at home when their defenders failed to clear the ball cleanly, leaving it bobbing all over the place in the 18-yard area. I was positioned near the penalty spot, when to my astonishment the ball landed on my favourite left foot. I just pulled the trigger and the ball flew into the top corner of the net. Fucking hell – how about that! I had scored my very first goal in the Football League, and I ran around like a nutter. It may have been the third goal in our 6–1 victory, but this was my initiation in the wonderful world of goal scoring.

If there can ever be a downside to scoring a goal, yours truly will find one though. As I celebrated my debut goal, I threw my arms aloft and caught my team-mate Bobby 'Shadow' Williams square on the chin with my elbow and knocked the poor bastard out cold. He needed lengthy treatment before he was allowed back on the pitch, but when he rejoined us he made sure he gave me grief at every possible opportunity. Did I care? Did I fuck! I'd scored a goal.

I wonder how I'd have felt that day had I known that in the not too distant future I would score the winning goal at Anfield in one of Liverpool's UEFA Cup wins. What I *do* know is that no goal can be sweeter than the first scored as a professional footballer.

It was a bloody marvel to be paid to play football, but being the new kid on the block I came in for some stick from my team-mates. They did me up like a kipper one night. Talk about green! I must have had 'naive twat' written across my forehead.

As usual, we had been working like dogs all day, but now it was time to enjoy a well-earned social gathering in the supporters' club. Coming from a family that included six boys, I enjoyed downing a pint or two. I was knocking them back with Dougie Hilliard and a crazy Scotsman called Alex Munro. Suddenly Alex came up with the idea we should have a drinking contest and, being of a competitive nature, I was well up for it. 'Let's see who can drink a pint the fastest,' he said, grinning.

Well, dozy Lloydie was desperate to impress these well-established older men. I also wanted to be embraced by the Bristol Rovers circle. So I was going to prove how macho I was! Twat! What a set-up I was walking into! And I didn't even twig when I kept on winning while drinking at a pretty average rate.

'I can't have a kid beat me in a drinking contest,' claimed Alex. 'Come on, let's do it again.'

This went on for four more rounds, and I don't need to tell you how pissed I was by now. I was out of my brains.

This could well have been the end of my career before it had even begun.

When Bert Tann found out, he went ballistic. I got the call to go and see him and I was literally quaking in my boots. He didn't see the funny side of it at all – probably because there wasn't one.

Alex and the lads might have thought it was funny, but the

manager told me if he ever caught me with a pint in my hand again I would be history. I made sure I never got caught again.

The fact that the caper had occurred in the supporters' club was probably what wound him up the most. His parting shot was: 'I've been appointed general manager, so I'll be moving upstairs soon. Your new manager will be Fred Ford, and I'll tell you this much, if you step out of line, he'll punch your teeth down your throat.'

I got the message.

And if my drinking habits had to change, then so did my diet. Times had changed. The war rations had long since disappeared and food was now plentiful – but it was the *kind* of food that was the issue.

I had always hated the vegetables Mum dished up, especially cabbage and sprouts. Ugh... it makes me gag even now when I think of it... smell it! But now, as a professional footballer, I needed strength – and that meant steak. Egg and chips was the staple diet of the rest of the family.

'How come favourite boy gets the steak when I'm the one who has been working his butt off all day? All *he* does is kick a football around the park,' my brother would grumble as he dipped his bread in his egg yolk.

I wasn't fazed. I didn't feel guilty about being the chosen one who was being dished up all the nourishing and tasty food. With hindsight, this surprises me, as we were a really close family who cared dearly about each other. But I reckon I must have been enjoying the attention. Ignoring the growls of my siblings, I'd clear my plate and then sit practising my autograph.

During my first season, which was 1967/68, I didn't even get as much as a sniff of first-team action – in fact, it was almost boringly uneventful. I was in the reserves, and that wasn't good enough as far as I was concerned. There was no such thing as a substitute then, so I didn't get a look in. The nearest was when I travelled to Southampton as the twelfth man, but in all honesty I'm sure I was only taken along for the experience. They had no intention of playing me.

I was frustrated and impatient, and in a quandary because I didn't want anyone in my beloved team to pick up an injury. I wanted us to win every single match – but there was a huge part of me desperate for the centre-half Stuart Taylor, who was consistently good and rarely picked up an injury, to break a leg and give *me* a break! He never did though. And he just wasn't the type to play dirty, and I don't think he ever picked up a suspension in his whole career.

An ideal scenario for someone like me, waiting not so quietly in the wings, is for your team to win 4–3, which usually meant your rival team-mate had given a crap performance, thus giving you a chance of getting off the damned bench. I know as far as loyalty goes you would expect me to say 4–0 because that means the defenders have kept a clean sheet, but I didn't want my rival to be solid in defence. I wanted him to fuck up so I could get a chance to prove myself and make the No.5 shirt all my own. Maybe some footballers will tell you different, but I don't think any footballer worth his salt should be content with parking his arse on the bench. Everyone should be fighting for their place in the first team.

Stuart Taylor was a good centre-half, but not great – he was too much of a gentleman to play in a defensive position at a high level. There was no room for gentlemen in defensive positions. I, on the other hand, was a hard, tough, fearless bastard who would tackle as if my life depended on it. A year later this 'hard bastard' attitude and rugged style of play was to attract the attention of Bill Shankly, and elevate me into First Division football. As far as Shankly was concerned, I ticked all the boxes – a thug with talent as well as brains who would work his arse off to get to the top.

My determination to get into Bristol Rovers' first team finally paid off, when canny old Fred Ford, our new team manager, came up with the brilliant idea of playing Stuart Taylor and I alongside each other to form the heart of the defence. I was six feet two inches, and at six feet five Stuart was a giant of a guy. We complemented each other perfectly – with my stronger left foot I automatically played left, and it was to be this strength that clinched my move to Liverpool the following season as the natural successor of the Merseyside legend left-footed Ron Yeats.

Thinking about it, Stuart and I should have been an awesome duo, a definitive brick wall, but the reality is we had limited success. Our goalie Laurie Taylor, who was a talented keeper, would often get caught out in no-man's land. It wasn't his fault. It couldn't have been much fun having us two giants darting around in front of him, blinding his view and confusing him. The poor fucker never knew whether to stay on his line or come out for a cross.

Our progress in the Third Division league table was mediocre, seeing us hover just below halfway, but the FA Cup was a different story. We had a fantastic run. Having disposed of Peterborough, Bournemouth, Kettering and Bolton Wanderers, we found ourselves up against the mighty Everton in the fifth round, away at Goodison Park. I was an excited young lad firing on all cylinders, and even though, in reality, we didn't have a hope of winning the FA Cup, you never know. In the FA Cup anything can happen. That's what makes this tournament so special.

An away trip to such a great side, win or lose, meant a nice fat wage packet. A draw away to a big club, with all those massive gate receipts, was a fantastic plus. But there was more than dosh at stake for me. This match against the Merseyside blues was to turn into a massive showcase for me. I had no idea then that Liverpool had been watching me in practically every game I'd played, and were interested to see how I would fare against Joe Royle. It's just as well – I think I would have died from fright had I known!

Joe was 19, the same age as me. He had already represented England. Like me, he was an all-round sportsman. We'd met before and it was great to meet up again. Lots of clubs were interested in buying him, including Manchester United, but Everton kept him in his local area by signing him. He was just sweet sixteen and, right up until 2005, when James Vaughan came along to take his crown, he held the record for being the youngest player to play for the club. He also held the record for being the youngest England player to score a goal until Michael Owen scored against Morocco in 1998. This gave him the edge over me, but I wasn't worried. We had locked horns five years before when I was playing for Bristol Boys and he for Liverpool Boys in the English Schools Trophy.

The FA Cup tie was played on a cold Wednesday night in February 1969. As a treat, we travelled up north the day before and booked into a hotel near Liverpool. On the morning of the match, after an easy training session, Fred Ford, who was a friend of Bill Shankly's, arranged for us to have a look around Melwood – Liverpool's training ground – and meet Shankly.

It was fucking awesome. For a boy like me, with less than two years' experience as a professional and having to train in the local park, going to Liverpool's training ground was amazing. My jaw literally dropped when I saw the facilities available to the boys at Anfield. It was evident that Shankly took immense pride in his training ground – he literally went on and on about it.

41

Looking back, I suppose the penny should have dropped! How come I didn't get wind of what was going on? What a divvy not twigging why I was being given so much attention! But I didn't – not even when Shankly stood next to me eyeing me up and down, before turning to Fred Ford and commenting, 'I didn't realise he was so tall. He's got it all really.'

Yes, it *really* should have clicked that I would soon be playing for the red side of Liverpool.

As for that massive FA Cup tie in front of 56,000 fans at Goodison Park, we gave a gritty performance, and it took Everton until 12 minutes before the whistle blew at the end of the match to score the only goal of the game.

And who was the goal scorer? None other than my rival Joe Royle. Blast! I was gutted the man I was designated to mark had scored a goal.

But I shouldn't have worried. The match had been watched exceptionally closely by Bill Shankly, who was apparently convinced once and for all that it was worth investing £55,000 for my services.

I wasn't to know this immediately. Instead I was kept in the dark until those in authority chose to disclose details of my transfer. Bristol Rovers had not finished with me yet. But it wasn't to be long before I was going to Anfield.

CHAPTER 6

OFF TO LIVERPOOL

DURING MY INITIAL talks with the great Liverpool manager Bill Shankly, he said to me, 'Larry, I've watched you play on several occasions, and have come to the conclusion that you would kick your grandmother for a fiver.'

My response was: 'I would actually kick her for half of that!'

He seemed impressed with my reply, and thus began our long and successful working alliance. Apparently, he was as impressed by my fighting attitude as he was by my tackling and aerial strength. He saw me as not only a natural replacement for Ron Yeats, but also an ideal partner for Tommy Smith in defence. They might not have been very happy about it, but the time was rapidly approaching when the golden oldies would have to step aside for new blood.

I still didn't fully understand how close I was to realising my dream of playing First Division football, but when I *did* find out I was as terrified as I was overjoyed. And when I learned Bill Shankly had me in mind to replace the legendary Ron Yeats, I was flabbergasted.

There was a strong bond between the Scotsmen at Liverpool Football Club during the sixties and seventies. Ron, along with Ian St John, was at the heart of Shankly's original powerhouse team. A team the Red Merseyside fans adored. Whereas Lloydie here had played the previous season in the side of a lowly Third Division team, and was an unknown quantity up north.

The local newspapers were full of stories about my impending move to Merseyside, but there was a wall of silence at Bristol Rovers. They were not ready to let me go just yet. Despite our great Cup run, we had fallen behind the rest of Division Three and were in danger of getting into a relegation dogfight.

It was Friday, 18 April 1969 and the final home league game of the season when it eventually came out into the open. The team sheet had been pinned to the notice board for the home game against Plymouth Argyle. I had played 43 league games that season so it was a shock to the system to read that I had been left out.

Being a hothead, I blew my top. I could get like that. Still can! But as I made my way to Fred Ford's office I was given the message *he* wanted to see *me*.

I stormed into his office, ready for one almighty row. 'Why have I been left out?' I fumed.

'You've been nursing a sore ankle all week.' Fred was as calm as I was heated.

'But it's all right now. It was only a minor injury anyway, and certainly not bad enough to miss a game.'

Fred stood firm. 'You can't play.'

'I can. I'm fit.' Steam was coming out of my ears by now.

Then Fred leaned forward in his chair and in a hushed voice told me, 'You can't play because it's important you don't aggravate the injury to your ankle.'

Above: School days – that's me, back row, fourth pupil from the left.

Below left: Me at thirteen.

Below right: Home in the garden in Bristol (*from left to right*) – Lanky Larry Lloyd, my little mum, my hero dad, and an elegant Sue.

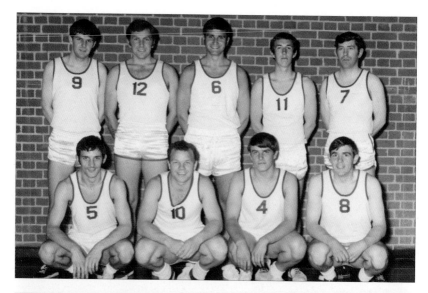

Above: Here I am (*back row, centre – how could you miss me?*) with the Wheatsheaf Basketball team, waiting for the day I turned pro with Bristol Rovers.

Below: Bristol Rovers, 1968. (*Back row, left to right*) Bobby Brown, Frank Prince, Stuart Taylor, Laurie Taylor, Me, Lindsay Parsons, Ray Mabbut; (*front row, left to right*) Ray Graydon, Vic Barney, Bobby Jones, Wayne Jones, Harold Jarman.

© *Bristol Evening Post*

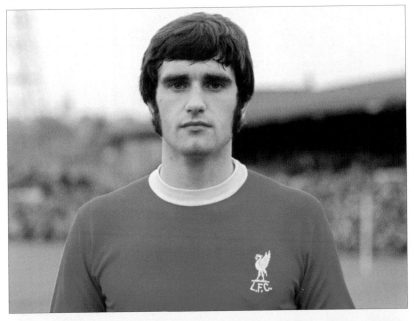

Above: Georgie Best eat your heart out – I wasn't too bad in my day! And as a Liverpool player I had the world at my feet.   © *Action Images*

Below: Liverpool '69: (*back row, l–r*) Geoff Strong, Gerry Byrne, Chris Lawler, Tommy Lawrence, Ray Clemence, me, Ian Ross, Alex Lindsay; (*front row l–r*) Ian Callaghan, Alun Evans, Roger Hunt, Tommy Smith, Ron Yeats, Emlyn Hughes, Ian St. John, Peter Thompson, Bobby Graham.   © *Cleva*

Above: England U23 international against West Germany in Leicester (*l–r*) – Ian Hutchinson (Chelsea), me, Mike Bernard (Stoke City), Ray Clemence (Liverpool).

© *Mercury Press Agency*

Below: With my fellow Liverpool boys after being selected to play for England (*l–r*) – me, Emlyn Hughes, Kevin Keegan and Ray Clemence.

© *Mercury Press Agency*

Above: In action for Liverpool against Arsenal in the 1971 FA Cup Final – winning a header… and clattering Peter Storey in the process! My first major defeat as a player hurt like hell. © *Cleva*

Below: Though winning the League and UEFA Cup double in 1973 more than made up for it! Here I am lifting the League championship trophy with the legendary Bill Shankly.

Above: With legendary goalkeeper Gordon Banks at a banquet after an international match against West Germany in 1972.   © *Helmut Heidak*

Below: Lloyd number 5 with Bob Paisley on the pitch at Wembley in '71. When Bob succeeded Shanks my days at Anfield were numbered, though that was down to my hot-headed nature more than anything – poor Bob wanted to keep me!

© *Cleva*

All smiles at Coventry City, but the smiles wouldn't last – my time
there was nothing short of a disaster!
© Cleva

Above: The dream-team pairing of Brian Clough and Peter Taylor saved me from certain obscurity at Coventry – and the glory days began!

© PA Photos

Below: The 1978-79 team photo. We started the season as champions and in the European Cup. (*Back row, l-r*) Ian Bowyer, Viv Anderson, Tony Woodcock, Kenny Burns; (*middle row, l-r*) trainer Jimmy Gordon, Frank Clark, me, Chris Woods, Peter Shilton, Colin Barrett, Cloughie; (*front row, l-r*) Peter Withe, David Needham, John McGovern, Martin O'Neill, John Robertson.

© PA Photos

I was about to protest again when the tone of his voice softened even more. 'Larry, if you want to go to Liverpool on Monday to sign for them, you must be fully fit.'

That heavy jaw of mine dropped again. 'Really?'

'Now get out of my office and behave yourself.'

The rest of the weekend passed in a blur. So it was true. I was going to sign for Liverpool. Can you imagine? Liverpool! Shit. The Sunday national newspapers were full of stories about the young Bristol Rovers boy who was going to replace the great Ron Yeats.

I remember sitting in the armchair at home, reading all about myself in the papers. I started wondering about that fan club again, and I definitely got rump steak that day.

Before I knew it, I was on the Monday-morning train to Liverpool – accompanied by general manager Bert Tann and local *Bristol Evening Post* reporter Robin Perry.

We arrived at Anfield just after one o'clock. I was a bloody nervous wreck, but that didn't stop my brain from working overtime. All the way from Lime Street station my mind was in a whirl.

A little later I was sitting on a wooden chair outside Bill Shankly's office, and wondering for the millionth time what wages I would ask for, when Emlyn Hughes, who was already in the England squad and therefore a household name, sat down next to me.

He'd been at the club since 1967, when Shanks had signed him as a teenager from Blackpool for a record fee for a full-back of £65,000. Now he was due to sign a new contract. 'Seems like a nice guy!' I thought to myself, as he shook my hand and wished me luck. How about that! I'm sitting next to Emlyn Hughes and soon he is going to be my team-mate. The whole idea of playing for Liverpool just wouldn't sink in.

Then another bloke appeared. It was Ron Yeats, the Liverpool captain I had been brought in to replace. He obviously knew this and it didn't exactly thrill him. His handshake was so firm that he nearly crushed my hand, and his glare told me he had no intention of giving up his place without a fight. The glint in his eye was menacing, but, hey, if Shankly thought I was up for the job, I would move hell and high water to grab that Liverpool No.5 shirt from him.

We sat there for absolutely ages – me and Emlyn. Shankly certainly knew how to get the message across that he was boss, and keeping us waiting was part of letting us know it.

Then suddenly I felt his presence. I was aware of his amazing aura even before he came into view. It was quite extraordinary. Emerging from his office, he threw his rich gravely Ayrshire voice in my direction and ordered me to follow him back inside.

There were no agents in those days, although that was soon to change. I think Kevin Keegan was one of the first to get an agent, but *I* certainly didn't have that luxury. (Mind you, over the years I've come to understand all about agents, and I'm not so sure they are a luxury anyway. I haven't got much time for them.)

So, what would be a fair and realistic salary to ask for? Hmm… My salary at Bristol Rovers had gone up to £20 a week with an additional £10 for an appearance in the first team in Bristol – a Third Division team who were struggling. I reckoned £100 a week plus bonuses wouldn't be too greedy a sum to request.

Sitting down opposite Shankly, I opened my mouth. But I was stopped in my tracks as he slapped a blue form down in front of me.

The form was totally blank! I looked at him – I think my expression was blank as well. He told me the terms verbally. 'You'll get thirty-five pounds a week basic, two pounds a point and five per cent of the transfer fee – to be spread over the four years of the contract.'

In effect I was getting five pounds a week rise. I was *well* gutted. He went on, his accent as strong as his manner, 'Larry, you will also receive, after tax, four payments of £450. This will be paid to you every July for the next four years.'

Speechless, I sat gawping for a moment or two, before I plucked up the courage to say, 'I was hoping for a bit more.'

'Sign now, or you can get the next train back to Bristol,' was the firm reply. There were to be no negotiations.

Now, what does an ambitious 20-year-old boy do in this position? Take the offered pen of course, and put your name on the dotted line pretty damn quickly. So, I signed a blank contract, and joined Liverpool FC.

Larry Lloyd felt as if he was floating around on Fantasy Island. I'd have actually signed for nothing. Any footballer in his right mind would, wouldn't they?

So there it was. I was a Liverpool player.

Bert Tann was a happy bunny as he hot-footed it back to Bristol with a £50,000 cheque burning a hole in his pocket, while reporter Robin Perry and I headed off to get a train to Southport to watch my old team play in their final league game of the season at Haigh Avenue. It was a strange feeling to no longer be a part of them. I was a Bristol boy and Bristol Rovers were in my blood. It was a disappointing match for the Rovers as they lost.

It was also a weird journey home on the team bus that spring day. My head was in a spin. Only a few hours before, I had been a Bristol Rovers boy – one of the lads – but now I was a Liverpool man, with legendary team-mates. I was also part of Shankly's plans to reorganise and build a new exciting Liverpool side.

I received mixed reactions from my Bristol mates. Some were envious, as *I* would have been had one of them been offered this chance of a lifetime. But the overall mood was one of jubilation as they wished me good luck.

On the journey back to Bristol, Fred Ford had let me in on a few secrets. It would appear that Liverpool hadn't been the only team interested in signing me. Both Manchester United and Fulham had made enquiries, but, for reasons known only to him, Fred had chosen not to tell me.

I was told, however, that one manager who I didn't impress was Tommy Docherty. The 'Doc' was managing Rotherham United at the time, and earlier in the season they had beaten us 3–2 at Millmoor. I remember I'd played a pig of a game. It had been one of my least effective days. After the game, Fred and 'Doc' were enjoying a pint, and Fred was telling him all about the interest in me, but 'Doc' scoffed at the news. 'That boy will never make it as long as I've got a hole in my arse,' he said.

Well, I hope his backside is OK, as he went on to have limited success as a big-time manager, while I have had it large and won every major honour in the game. Don't get me wrong, Tommy Docherty is a legend – but I'm mighty pleased he got it wrong about me.

Leaving Bristol Rovers was sad. There is always such a love affair you have with your home club, and till this day I still look out for Bristol Rovers' results at five o'clock on a Saturday afternoon.

But in 1969 it was excitement all the way to Anfield, and I was more than ready to pull on that red shirt!

I made my debut for Liverpool just 48 hours after signing. OK, it was only for the reserves, but this was to be expected, as this was the Liverpool way. We travelled to Nottingham Forest (a team I was to enjoy great success with seven years later, when they dominated not only this country, but also Europe).

This was a tremendously busy time for me, not only

professionally, but also personally. My fiancée Sue and I had already made plans to marry the following summer after we had saved enough money. But the transfer and 'signing on' fee gave us an option to bring the wedding forward by 12 months, and we jumped at the chance. We were very much in love. I might have been a bruiser with my boots on, but was a romantic when it came to matters of the heart. However, we still had to find a different church, a new venue for the reception and much more besides!

Sue was a beauty with her dark curls, fine features and trim figure, and I couldn't wait to make her my wife. She was an intelligent and smart girl who was dedicated to her studies. Being two-thirds of the way through her training to be a State Registered Nurse (SRN), we needed to find a hospital in Liverpool that would take her on for her final year. It was tricky at first and we were getting into a right panic but then Walton Hospital came to the rescue.

It was quite some upheaval, but we were young and energetic, and our hearts were full of ambition and confidence. We gave our families just three weeks' notice about the wedding, and our move north.

Sue and I had met at school where we had been in the same class, and I'd carried her books home from school. She had known me since I was a young boy dreaming of making the big time, so she knew how much it meant to me. I guess back then we had it all. Well, except for a home – which was pretty important, really.

Bill Shankly couldn't have been more against us bringing the marriage forward. He gave us a really hard time. He believed we were far too young to get hitched and, more importantly, thought I should be concentrating totally on my football.

But I was adamant, and when he realised I wasn't budging he gave in and from then on couldn't have been more helpful.

Shankly and Liverpool Football Club came to the rescue and

fixed us up with a house in Maghull. Liverpool were (and I'm certain still are) extremely helpful to their staff and players.

Peter Robinson was secretary then, and he offered us a club house at a minimal rent. It was neat and tidy and had been very well kept.

But Sue, like most women, wanted it decorated to her liking – and quite rightly so. Yet this wish turned into a fiasco, led by Shanks himself. By God, that man knew what he wanted and got it by whatever means he could. I guess that was why he was so successful.

It was a beautiful summer's day when Sue and I travelled from Bristol to Liverpool in our new second-hand Ford Cortina, which we had bought with my 'signing on' fee, for a meeting with the decorator at the club. The idea was to look through different colour schemes. We were a bit thrown to see Shankly standing there with the decorator, but I simply introduced him to Sue and then turned my attention to the job at hand.

As we turned the pages and mused over what we did and didn't like, Shanks hovered around. Every now and again he threw an interested glance over our shoulders. To be honest, he was making me nervous. If he was this intense about colour schemes and wallpaper patterns, what the hell was he going to be like about tackles, passes, defending and attacking? I guess I must have lingered too long on a page that was predominantly blue, because suddenly, out of the corner of my eye, I could see Shanks stomping about the room, muttering to himself.

After about an hour he snapped. It had all become too much for him. In two enormous strides he was beside us, and in that deep accent he informed Sue and I, in no uncertain terms, that the house was to be red and white. And he added angrily, 'It will certainly not be blue, because *that*,' he spat, 'is the colour of "*that* other team" across Stanley Park.'

What a bloody waste of a trip! Our front door was probably always going to be red, and the paintwork a gleaming white. The garage door was also painted red. All it needed was a white picket fence and red roses climbing the walls to finish off the 'Anfield House'. And there were to be no shades of blue anywhere – not until you reached the other side of Stanley Park, where the Evertonians hung out.

I learned quickly of both Shanks's loyalty to his club, and his extreme dislike of the opposition. Loyalty was a theme in Liverpool.

A few weeks later, I had to return to Liverpool to see the decorator again – only this time I went alone, and by train.

On arriving at Lime Street Station I hailed a taxi. I climbed into the back seat and asked the driver if he knew where Anfield was. The driver swivelled around and threw me an odd look. When he answered he might as well have been talking in double-dutch, because I couldn't understand a bloody word he said. I tell you, the Liverpudlian accent takes some getting used to! Wide-eyed and wearing an incredulous expression, he spoke ten to the dozen. Then he set off, so I guessed he *did* know the way. Jeeesus, he rabbited on and on all the way to Anfield. His speech was interrupted from time to time with intermittent guffaws of laughter, and suddenly the penny dropped. He was telling jokes. He spat a lot, and I was grateful to be out of spitting distance. He also kept referring to 'the Geeermans' – which I guessed must be the Germans. It was all lost on me – a boy from down Bristol way.

When we reached Anfield he spat again… and I ducked!

'You're the young lad who Shankly has just signed to take over from Ron Yeats, aren't you?'

I was amazed he'd guessed. But I was learning fast that Liverpool fans knew everything there was to know about their mighty team. When I said, 'Yes, I am,' he refused to take any money for my fare.

But then he warned me, 'Ron is a Liverpool hero, and you've got a bloody hard job on your hands.' Then he threw a cheeky smile at me and said, 'Remember my face, because one day I'm going to be a star too. My name is Stan Boardman and I'm a comedian.' He certainly was, and he did indeed go on to be very successful.

Now it was time to settle down and get stuck in! Sue and I moved into our house a week or so before I was due to report for my first pre-season training with the mighty Liverpool. These were special days for me and my new wife. When we weren't getting the house straight or finding our way around the area, we spent long lazy afternoons watching movies.

There were many perks to being a Liverpool football player. The locals would do pretty much anything to get their hands on a match ticket. Butchers would trade the best steaks and chops for a chance to spend a Saturday afternoon on the Kop. It seemed to me a Scouser loved a deal almost as much as they loved their team.

As for me – I was about to be a great big part of the Kop.

The first morning at Anfield was surreal. Legends were milling around everywhere, interspersed with us new kids on the block. It was very much 'us and them', and there was definitely some bad feeling on the part of the older and well-established players. Ian St John, Geoff Strong and Ron Yeats didn't take too kindly to the situation.

There was a hell of a lot of resentment in the dressing room. It was a club of cliques then. There was the Scottish clan led by Yeats and St John and the Scouse group of Tommy Smith, Chris Lawler and Ian Callaghan. Professionals like Tommy Lawrence, Chris Lawler, Ian Callaghan and Peter Thompson were brilliant – true diamond blokes. I especially admired Roger Hunt. What a player! I had watched him play alongside the other 1966 World Cup heroes, and now here I was, sharing the air he breathed. He encouraged and inspired us. He bore no malice whatsoever, and was a true gent.

CHAPTER 7

THE SMALLEST CHAPTER FOR THE SMALLEST FAN CLUB

'THE LARRY LLOYD Fan Club' was set up by an obsessive fan of mine. How about that? All that practising of my autograph around the dinner table as a kid was necessary after all. I couldn't wait to tell my brothers and sisters their bro had become a heart-throb.

I'll let you into a secret though – you could have held a meeting in a telephone box! I think I had two fans… or was it one? She loved me anyway; at least I hope it was a 'she'. I heard my picture was on her bedroom wall. Fuck me – imagine choosing to go to bed with my mug staring down at you! Mind you, I have heard it said that in my prime, with my long black sideburns and exquisite dress sense, I resembled George Best. I think Georgie had a few more fans in his club!

Anyway, moving swiftly on to a legend, and icon, my old boss Bill Shankly.

CHAPTER 8

BILL SHANKLY AND MY LIVERPOOL DAYS

'He came to Liverpool, he built a team, he brought alive his Glenbuck dream, and Anfield, his adopted home, made sure he never walked alone.'

LAST VERSE OF A POEM BY DON GILLESPIE ENTITLED 'REMEMBER GLENBUCK'

BILL SHANKLY MADE Liverpool his home for an incredible 21 years – from 1959 until 1974. When he arrived, the club was struggling and morale was low. He was instantly at home, and this was probably because the people of Merseyside reminded him of his roots in the small hillside village of Glenbuck, Ayrshire. Like me, he was one of ten children and, like me, he idolised his father. But, whereas I was the only Lloyd brother to play professional football (despite my brother Ivan reckoning he was better than me), all four of the Shankly boys played professional football – either in England or Scotland.

It has been said that he sensed the kinship of the supporters straight away. He connected with their passion and enthusiasm. If it is true that Liverpool is like a religion, I have the distinct feeling that it was in 1959 when it all began – with the arrival of the spirited Bill Shankly.

Shanks brought much experience of his early footballing days to the Liverpool team. His past has much to do with why he is regarded by many as being the greatest football manager in the history of the game.

It has been said that Bill's life was shaped by 'the harshness of a hard-working mining community'. He was brought up surrounded by hard-working, passionate men who stood firm by their beliefs. He'd watched his elders struggle throughout the General Strike in 1926 and experienced his father's fury as they were sold out by the politicians and those in positions of power. The miners stood firm but eventually had no choice but to return to the mines through starvation.

He learned early on not to trust those in positions of power. This sense of mistrust was to shadow him all through his life and often lead him into hot water with those in authority.

He couldn't help but take politics seriously as his whole young world was caught up in the terrible deadly conditions the miners had to face every day. Every time there was an accident the entire community was caught up in the drama, and every day every single one feared for their own or their loved ones' safety.

He was a fan of the great Scottish poet and socialist Robbie (pronounced 'Rabbie') Burns, and by the time he had grown into manhood he had taken on board all his early childhood messages about the importance of teamwork. Of course, he took these deeply ingrained beliefs into his sporting life.

His father, although a tailor by trade, was an excellent athlete. Bill, like his brothers, worked for periods of six days a week down a mine, but come Sunday they would relish the fresh air and enjoy playing football.

He told me that lots of the villagers became professional footballers, even though the population was small. It would seem that it was this harsh, almost austere lifestyle that fuelled the footballing fervour in Bill Shankly and his fellow villagers. The village team was called Glenbuck Cherry Pickers, and Bill's father had been a player in the team before his son. A fascinating aspect of their tactics and work ethic was reflected in how Shankly managed Liverpool. These men who faced death every day down the mineshaft found it natural to join together in team spirit.

Allegedly, the strength of the team of Glenbuck was greater than the sum of its parts, thus providing a string of professional and international players, and the experience of playing for the Cherry Pickers taught Shankly a hell of a lot.

There was one more passion that he absorbed into his ever-growing strength of character, and that was his love of the cinema. It was his father who introduced him to the American movie heroes of the day – Jimmy Cagney and Edward G Robinson. Even as a young boy he could identify with these legends.

I remember once, when he was having a go at us in the dressing room, he threw some photographs down on the table and yelled over to Tommy Smith, 'You think you're hard. You're not a hard man. You've got it easy. If one of this lot stepped out of line, they were shot.'

When we played away, we always had to be checked into our hotel in time for him to watch *The Untouchables* on TV. When I think about it now, I realise he was very obsessive – perhaps he had that obsessive compulsive disorder that David Beckham has!

His father, having been a tailor, also instilled in him the importance of a smart suit. He wore a suit well did Shankly. He used to strut around, giving it large, with his hands on his hips like a gangster. It makes me really laugh when I look back on his whole demeanour.

There can be no doubt that Bill Shankly was one of the all-time great managers, not a great coach in my opinion, but a huge motivator. I believe his bark was definitely worse than his bite, but there were many sides to this complex man. Sometimes he could be quite menacing, but at other times very funny. Even the way he spat his words at us was a carbon copy of James Cagney. He was scary but not really scary at the same time, because part of it felt like he was acting.

Oh! How he could tell a story to great effect. Immediately prior to big matches he would slag off other teams terribly. It didn't matter who it was – Leeds, Manchester United… whoever – they all got the Shankly treatment. When we played Manchester United he'd say, 'They've only got George Best, Denis Law and Bobby Charlton – if you can't beat three players in a duff team you need shooting. Because they're all United has got.'

I remember one fixture when Ipswich came to Anfield. It was hilarious. He looked the opposition up and down and then at quarter to three (just before kick-off), he told us to take our shirts off and put them by the door. He said he was going to throw the shirts on to the pitch. 'I've just had a sneak peak at the Ipswich team and they're a joke. One's got bandy legs. Another is wearing black trousers with brown shoes, and another poor sod is wearing glasses so thick he can't possibly see the ball. Blind as a bat, he must be! The shirts can beat them on their own.'

Well, as you can imagine, any pre-match nerves were dispelled in an instant. All that knotting up of the stomach went and we would run out on to the pitch feeling we could take on the world.

Another example of Shanks's type of motivation occurred one Friday lunchtime during a team talk. We were at the training ground sitting around a small magnetic football pitch with magnetic men. One set of players were in red (us, of course) and the others were all in white. We were due to play Leeds the following day, and Shanks was in the process of laying the white team in the formation they were likely to play in the following day. After about ten minutes of ranting and raving, his right-hand man Bob Paisley calmly pointed out to the manager that Leeds had only ten men on the board. After a few seconds' thought, he opened his hand and there sitting in his palm was the eleventh man. He looked at the number of this player, which happened to be No.7, a shirt worn by the great Peter Lorimer. Then, with all the strength he could muster, he threw the magnetic figure at the closed window, shattering the glass, and the miniature Lorimer went flying through it. Shanks was shouting, 'He can't fucking play anyway.'

There were other incidents that showed his personality. We were travelling on the team bus across Europe to play in a competition when we hit a major traffic jam. Now at times like this, Shankly was at his absolute worst. He had no patience whatsoever. Time was passing and we weren't moving. We didn't know whether there had been a road traffic accident, or whether road works was the problem.

The driver decided to get off the bus to investigate the hold-up.

Shankly's impatience was growing by the second and he began to pace up and down the aisle, muttering all the time about how late we were going to be. Then he lost it big style. He was so uptight he didn't realise what he was saying. He had to take his frustration out on someone, so the driver got it. 'Will you tell that fucking driver to get back on the bus or we're going without him!'

Tommy Smith, who had been a successful local school football player, was taken to Anfield in 1959 by his mother, who sensed her son was destined for big things. Therefore, he had seen all there was to see, and knew all there was to know, by the time I arrived on the scene, and he knew Shanks inside out. He was always telling us other funny stories about our manager.

Tommy told one story that tickled me. Shankly went into the opposition's dressing room about half an hour before we were due to kick off. He went on the pretext of wishing them all the best for the game. He didn't mean a word of it, but while he was in there his eyes scanned the players and he noted everything worth noting. Then, minutes later he came back to the Liverpool players and said, 'Now look here. It's all going wrong for them. One's got his ankle strapped up and another's got a bandage on his elbow.'

Of course, none of this was true, but the lie always managed to calm our nerves.

Shanks really was full of this bravado all the time. He was also an amateur psychologist. He had ways of disarming and calming raging players who went to him with a grievance – they went into his office with the hump and came out feeling a whole lot better. His man-management skills really were superb.

The working alliance between him and his right-hand man Bob Paisley was second to none. The added special ingredient of Joe Fagan, who took great care of the reserves, ensured a magical unison. And what was so brilliant was the management never had favourites.

When Bill Shankly signed me, he also signed Alec Lindsay, Steve Heighway and Ray Clemence. In the years between 1965 and 1969, he signed Emlyn Hughes, Alun Evans and Tony Hateley. Before these additions, there had been a long period of no signings while Shanks played Ian St John and Ron Yeats, men he had admired for a long time and had dreamed of having in his team. The lads hadn't let him down, and they brought domestic glory back to the club in the mid-sixties.

From 1968 to 1970, during a transitional period of dropping the older players and building the newer team, Liverpool had a bad spell where no trophies were won. There was a lot of speculation in the press and among the supporters about whether they could remain successful during the change-over period, and quite rightly so.

The team hit rock bottom in the 1969/70 season during an FA Cup quarter-final match against Watford at Vicarage Road. Watford humiliated them with a 1–0 defeat and Shankly flew into action.

Out went St John, Hunt, Yeats and Lawrence, and in came the new stars – me, Clemence, Hall, Lindsay and Heighway.

If the story is true, the reason Bill Shankly kept his original players in the team for so long was for personal reasons. Apparently, it went back to his own playing days when he believed he had been put on the shelf far too early. He felt deeply hurt about this as he felt certain he still had plenty to give the game.

One day, when training as usual with both the established older players and my new peers, Shankly decided to surprise us by announcing we were going to have a practice match. The first team were to play the reserves, and of course I was in the latter team marking none other than Roger Hunt.

After about 15 minutes, Roger received the ball just inside our half, turned and ran at me. I only knew one way to tackle, and that was to go in hard and try to win the ball. As I was keen to impress the watching Shankly and Bob Paisley, I was perhaps a little too enthusiastic with my tackle. I totally mistimed it and sent Roger ten feet up in the air. He did a double flip before landing awkwardly on his shoulder. It seemed to me to take forever for him to recover, and during this tense time I took unmerciful stick from Tommy Smith and Ian St John. 'You can't do that to Roger Hunt!' they cried in unison. *Sorry, pals, I just did!*

The 'friendly' continued, and later, during a break in play, Roger came up to me and astonished me by saying, 'I heard some of the boys having a go at you. Don't take any notice, son. Just keep doing what you're doing and you'll do well. I tell you, Larry – I'm already having second thoughts about coming near you again, and I'm the bravest player you could meet. Imagine the effect you are going to have on the less brave. Well done.'

That was a huge moment for a youngster like me. There were some stupid things said to me during my career, and I learned quickly that negative shit needs to be discarded for the rubbish it is. But what the great Roger Hunt said to me that day stayed with me throughout my career.

He said he loved the way I took possession at the back and was sharp enough to suss the best way forward to attack. He added that it was such a plus for the team because I gave them confidence to push forward quickly as soon as the ball hit my trusty left foot.

Yes, Roger Hunt has a special place in my memory bank.

My Liverpool debut came much sooner than I expected. Remember me saying how much us players hope and pray for the number-one player to get an injury and allow the number two to get a game? Well, it happened to me when captain and Kop hero Ron Yeats suffered a back injury, which meant I was on my way to play against West Bromwich Albion at The Hawthorns. I remember the day well – with terror!

At five to three, I looked over to see the terrifying sight of the legendary Jeff Astle warming up; I was literally sick with nerves. My great big hairy legs were shaking like jelly, as all the strength drained from me. I, the boy from Bristol, had been designated to mark Astle, a man I knew to be a big, strong, old-fashioned centre-forward who was an international with hundreds of league games under his belt. To say Lloydie was terrified is a massive understatement.

Remember, I was only 20 years of age and had only played 40 games in the Third Division, plus a dozen for the Liverpool reserves. Quite some difference! But I was going to give it my best shot – even if my legs were about to part company with my brain. Newspapers had screamed headlines like: 'Lloyd Must Shackle Astle'. How the hell was I supposed to do that? I kept reminding myself of the words Bill Shankly had told Fred Ford, 'I like him. He's the right build; he's brave and good in the air. What with his brilliant left foot, he's everything I need at Anfield.'

Well, my brain kicked into gear with that memory and I kept telling myself I must be careful not to be dragged out of position. With this in mind, I decided wherever Astle went I would go too.

I never left that man's side for 90 minutes. (I must have played well because I was selected to play my home debut the following week against Nottingham Forest.) But, to this day, that very first game for Liverpool marking Astle is a blur.

There's a funny story here, though, because many years later I met up with him, and he laughed, 'Larry, you were a pain in the arse that day. I reckon, if I'd decided to leave the pitch and go for a crap, you would have come with me and sat in the next cubicle.' He was right.

Those two snatched matches while Ron was injured were a great learning curve. I learned that once I'd stepped out into the bright lights it was horrible going back into the shadows in the reserves. But what I also learned was that I could keep up with the big boys. In fact, I had become a big boy myself, which was just as well because there were some huge matches coming my way.

I was also being compared with the legendary Jack Charlton. The media were saying I had the potential to be as good as him, and I was determined to prove them right.

DERBY DAY AND I'M PLAYING

I had been steadily working my way into the first team and by 1970 I was deemed ready to play in a local Liverpool v Everton derby. Derby day anywhere, in any sport, is always a passionate affair; but till this day I had never ever experienced anything quite like the Merseyside derby. Liverpool versus Everton matches are very special events for the passionate people of Liverpool. The atmosphere builds in the city from the previous Saturday's match and all local talk is focused on it.

The media are in a frenzy all the time. Newspapers and television stations report on anything and everything, including interviews with fans, players and managers. Families and friends are divided, and it is quite amazing that these days pass with little or no serious trouble.

My first taste of derby day was unbelievably exciting as well as nerve wracking for me and the other youngsters in the team. The noise of the 54,000 crowd was deafening as the six of us made our derby debuts. There was Alec Lindsay, Brian Hall, John McGlaughlan, Steve Heighway, John Toshack and, of course, young Lloydie. It was good to share such a phenomenal experience with my new mates. It was also good to share the nerves around!

The more experienced Everton side took an early two-goal lead – which didn't help those nerves. The Blues were on cloud nine at half-time, but we were on a different kind of cloud – a black one – fully expecting Shanks to give us a bollocking. But he didn't. In the style of the then England manager Sir Alf Ramsey, he calmly told us we were the better side and if we settled down we would win. They were lucky, he reckoned, to be in the lead.

Wow! This was a different Shanks to the one who usually shouted and screamed while steam came out of his ears – but it worked. We were stupendous in the second half. John Toshack, who had recently joined us from Cardiff, became the new hero of the Kop by scoring twice to level the game, 2–2. But there was more. As the noise rose to levels I'd never heard before, Chris Lawler crashed the winner in from close range to score one of the most important goals of his career. Liverpool erupted and, depending on whether they were red or blue, people were going crazy with either delight or despair. What a day!

We were not the greatest Liverpool team, but we kept the club right up there and won a few things. When I went into the side it was the only time four or five players were replaced in one hit. Since then it has been one in and one out. There is no doubt I was a part of the biggest reshuffle ever.

Things were really going well for me in every way. My football was improving all the time, which raised my confidence levels no end. Sue and I had also settled in well in our little house, and were enjoying married life big time. She had met a lot of good friends – we both had – and our feeling of domestic bliss rose to ecstatic levels with the arrival of our daughter Yolanda, who was born at 7pm on 22 October 1970 in Fazakerley Hospital. Sue had a difficult labour and a few days later her baby blues weren't made any easier when pictures appeared in the local newspaper of me modelling some leatherwear with a topless Miss Liverpool.

Well, someone had to do it! A cracker she was as well, but, unlike Georgie Best, I would never have dreamed of taking it further. Honest to God, it just never entered my mind. It was just a bit of harmless fun. I suppose with that great thing called hindsight I was a bit thoughtless to pose with a model while Sue was giving birth to our first child. Then again, compared to the revelations in today's tabloids about what professional footballers get up to with prostitutes and the like, I reckon my spot of modelling was rather tame.

Anyway, my moment of enjoyment with Miss Liverpool cost me dearly as Sue insisted I buy her a leather coat to make up for the pain and misery. The wives and girlfriends of the players were as competitive then as the likes of Posh Beckham and her peers of today.

Sue, having finished her studies and now a qualified SRN, struck up friendships with some of the other players' wives. She enjoyed the whole footballers' wives scene, and being young and pretty she looked a picture in her hot-pants and other fashions of the early seventies. She got on really well with Ray Clemence's wife, Veronica. She also liked Rhona Ross, wife of Ian Ross, and also Roy Evans's better half, Mary. Being of a similar age group, they had lots in common. She liked the football scene and understood the enormity of what my career meant to me.

Our house was in a cul-de-sac, and we had some smashing neighbours, which was a relief because, being far from her hometown, Sue could have been very lonely during my long hours away training and playing. We had some special neighbours called Bill and Rita. Rita became like a grandmother to Yolanda.

When you're a footballer and you play for a club like Liverpool, you receive (both as a club and individuals) hundreds of invitations to attend various functions.

As a rule, Shankly hated his players going out at night, but one night he decided we should all attend with our wives. There were a lot of new faces at the club, so he must have thought that this was an ideal opportunity for everyone to mix. The idea fell as flat as a pancake, as the younger element wanted to stick together, and the golden oldies had no intention whatsoever of slumming it with what they considered the small fry.

Now, if there was a part of football life that I found amusing, it was what today is termed the 'WAGs', the wives and girlfriends of the footballers. As this particular evening at the function progressed, on my way to the toilet, I was confronted by a woman that someone had pointed out earlier as Ron Yeats's wife.

She asked me, 'Are you that new boy Larry Lloyd?'

I said I was.

'Is it right that you have been brought in to replace Ron?'

'That could be a possibility in time,' I said. I was being tactful for a change.

'Well, let me tell you something, young man [*young man!!*], you have no chance. You are simply not in his class.'

Hmm... Charming. Welcome to Liverpool. But at least I knew where I stood with *that* particular female, which I suppose has its upside. I think.

Mrs Yeats was not the only female to show her undivided loyalty to her man. Footballers' wives seem to me to be very blinkered – but who can blame them. There's a lot at stake, especially nowadays when they can actually become a celebrity in their own right, for basically doing sweet fuck all! The bit that I find hysterical is that, despite some of them having never *seen* a football match before dating their man, they suddenly become experts on the game. Nuts!!

Another thing that made me smile was the ladies' pampering sessions on the morning before a game. Hours before going to the game, they would be having their hair and nails done, and after carefully applying their make-up would agonise in front of the mirror for an eternity while trying to make up their minds what outfit they would wear.

Matches were the showcase to parade their designer clothes. It was such a hoot to watch them all sitting around in their finery, as they tried, usually without success, to discuss accurately the finer points of the game.

I was living the dream and I wanted this dream to go on forever and a day. Living life to the full and giving my football everything. Well, not quite everything. Something was about to happen to make me sit up and re-evaluate the meaning of life.

CHAPTER 9

GROWING UP OVERNIGHT

MY LOVELY DAD, whom I had always totally worshipped, had been ill for quite some time when I received the chilling message that he was coming to the end of his days. He had always had heart problems, then the cancer had got him, and finally his dicky heart gave up.

Anyone who has lost a loved one to a long lingering illness knows the misery and desperation of watching them slowly wither away and finally leave you. But the strange thing is, however ill they have become, the end still comes as a shock.

It was a bitterly cold Sunday morning in mid-December 1970 when Sue and I loaded up our car and headed down to Bristol with baby Yolanda. It was a five-hour journey down the M6 so it was about midday when we arrived. After being told how desperately ill he was, I felt relieved he was able to hold his little granddaughter for a short time. That Sunday was so very special. My memories of us all together will stay with me forever. Dad was so weak, but there was no way he wasn't going to hold Yolanda. My poor blind dad was missing out on yet another vision of splendour, but holding her and smelling her sweet baby aroma meant everything to him, and he was so overwhelmed he began to cry.

He wasn't the only one to lose control of his emotions. I was 21 years old and felt I was too young to be saying goodbye to my dad. Tears were streaming down my face, as I knew how overjoyed he was that he'd had the opportunity to hold my little girl before he died. We had been such a big family of boys, so Yolanda was very special indeed.

In the early hours of Monday morning, I was woken by my brother Adrian. 'Larry, come downstairs quickly. I think Dad might have died.'

I went to Dad's bedside and stood there looking down at him for a very long time. I had never seen a dead person before, but I knew he had gone. The doctor came and confirmed the death and they took him away. I never went to see him in the Chapel of Rest. I didn't see the point.

That poor old man had withered away during his illness and he wasn't the man I recognised as my dad. My dad had once been a big, strong, handsome man, and that was the man I was grieving for. I had to find a way of believing he had gone to a better place and, importantly, he was finally out of pain. I imagined him looking down with pride at the family he and my mother had raised, knowing he'd done a damn good job. The doctor told me my dad had often spoken to him about me, and said he was certain he'd been clinging on to life waiting to meet Yolanda and say goodbye to me.

In a totally irrational outburst, I screamed, 'I wish I hadn't come. If I'd stayed away he would still be here.' But I knew deep down this was nonsense and, of course, the doctor told me as much. It was my father's time; it was as simple as that.

We had an old black lab called Jibbo. Like many dogs he was very intuitive. He had been with us for 15 years, and as he got older he rarely left my dad's side. Jibbo was not an official guide dog for the blind, he was simply our family pet, but he really was quite incredible. It was quite something to be able to witness him protecting my dad. If he got up to go to the bathroom, Jibbo would often nudge him away from the coffee table or steer him away from any other obstacle. I guess you could say he was a self-taught guide dog. I often shake my head in wonderment when I think about the lives my dad touched, and not only humans – because the day my dad died, old Jibbo walked out of the house and was never seen again.

My family and I buried Dad, and then it was time for me to go back up north, and get back to the normality of playing football. I grew up very quickly at Liverpool. I held a responsible position, and the prying eyes of the media were never far away.

As the 1969/70 season drew to a close, Shankly told me that win, lose or draw I was going to play in all six end-of-season matches. He wanted me to have a good run in the team before the summer. I was ecstatic. Shankly was in full flow, chopping and changing the team, and trying to suss out which of us was most up to the job.

One senior player who was still a regular in the side was Ian St John, Ron Yeats's great pal. You could say that he and I weren't on the best of terms. During the half-time break of one of these final matches – and one in which St John was having a pig of a game – the Scotsman decided to have a right old pop about me. 'Ron should be playing,' moaned St John. '*His* –' he threw an evil eye in my direction '– defensive headers aren't finding any of his team-mates.'

Well, as any centre-half will tell you, when a ball is tossed into the penalty area and you are challenged by a six-foot centre-forward, you are just happy to win the ball and head it away from the danger zone.

Shanks turned on St John: 'Lloyd is doing his job exactly the way I want him to do it. You, on the other hand, need to work harder to pick up the loose balls.' What Shanks was doing was bringing the message home loud and clear to the older players that, like it or not, changes were going to be made, and they either accepted this or they moved on. I must say, though, that Ron Yeats, who had a couple of games at left-back, was eventually totally supportive of me. After his initial period of being pissed off by my arrival, it was a great relief to me that we got on well.

I can't blame Ian St John for being prickly. I was yet to experience the dreadful feeling of your playing career coming to an end. It really is a wretched feeling. Way back in 1959 (just when Tommy Smith's mum was walking him through the Anfield gates), St John, then a Motherwell player, scored one of the fastest hat-tricks on record. Having begun his career north of the border, he was soon on his way to Liverpool on a £30,000 fee – twice as much as the previous highest transfer fee. In his first match for the Reds, he managed to score another hat-trick, and, although it was an important derby match against the Blues that they ended up losing, St John had arrived in great style. He peaked somewhere in the mid-1960s, but by the time he was in his thirties his fitness levels were dipping somewhat. He had been a prolific goal scorer in a team he adored and, by the time he was complaining about the likes of me, he had scored more than a hundred goals for his team.

Joe Fagan was my mentor during that first difficult season at Anfield. One day he pulled me aside and told me that Bill Shankly was delighted with the way I had improved, and that I should look after myself during the summer, as the No.5 shirt had my name on it the following season. Chuffed to bits, me, Sue and little Yolanda headed off to Majorca – a place that was to become a firm favourite during the years to come – especially during my Nottingham Forest days.

My friendship with Joe Royle began in earnest during this holiday. He and his wife were staying at the same resort as us, and we got in the habit of meeting up at the same beach-bar every morning, where we would chat about... hmm... let me think! Ah! Football. Football and our futures on Merseyside, where we knew we would be fighting for our teams across Stanley Park. Had Shankly realised what firm pals we were becoming, he would have gone berserk! But I was more than capable of being good friends off the pitch, but enemies on the turf.

Tommy Smith was a very big personality. I think I would describe him as a rough diamond – and I mean that as a compliment. A ruggedly handsome man, he was a big presence both on and off the pitch. Once he'd earned his reputation of being a hard man, he was sharp enough to hold on to his label. At 15 years of age, he was there at the beginning of Bill Shankly's reign and was caught up in those first glorious days. Needless to say, he was idolised by the fans, and the boy who had served a two-year apprenticeship, raking over top soil on the pitch, was a first-team favourite. Never believe he was a hard man with no skills, though. Tommy had great ability, and was a great all-rounder. But it was the nickname 'Iron Man' that stuck during the unbelievable 633 games he played for Liverpool.

Although many of Tommy Smith's opponents might disagree with my description of him, he was basically a man with a heart of gold. He was a diamond most of the time, except one day in training when there was, um… an incident. Those same opponents, I dare say, would recognise the following Tommy Smith behaviour.

We were training, and playing a five-a-side game when I passed the ball to him a little too firmly. He couldn't get to the ball, which infuriated him, and, fuck me, did he let me know it!

Now, like most of us big lads, Tommy was conscious of his weight. So, when I shouted, 'Run for it, you fat bastard,' he wasn't too happy. The training ground went deathly silent, because no one dared say that to Tommy. The rest of the players stood still as Tommy thundered towards me and asked, 'What did you say Lloyd?'

I knew instantly this was to be a defining moment for my relationship with the boys, who now stood gawping. I was still a reasonably new kid on the block and, being a big lad and defender, I immediately knew I couldn't back down. So I stood tall, repeated the abuse and received an almighty clump across my ear. I got one back on his nose before Peter Cormack, who was probably one of the smallest players in the team, jumped in between us. Bravery indeed, because I'm afraid poor Peter came away from the scuffle worse than either Tommy or me. It was total chaos – like something out of the Keystone Cops.

Bob Paisley immediately called a halt to training, and as we walked off the pitch Tommy yelled over to me, 'You're going to get an axe through your fucking front door tonight.'

He frightened the living daylights out of me. But nothing happened of course. Thank God. After he'd calmed down, he knew better than to carry out his threat, and we ended up the best of pals.

Once, when Tommy was leaving a match at Anfield, he was approached by a couple. Liverpool had been playing Preston at home, and, seeing the man and woman standing in his path, he asked, 'Can I help you?'

'We just want to thank you for not kicking our son. He was playing inside-left, and we were so worried for his safety.'

I think they left Tommy speechless – now, there's a first!

I have a lot to be grateful to Tommy Smith for – because that generous guy, who was four years my senior, taught me a great deal in footballing terms.

When Shanks took the captaincy off Tommy and handed it to Emlyn Hughes during the 1971/72 season, it became out-and-out war between the two. It was the mother of all clashes between the old guard and the new boy on the block.

The rivalry between the two bubbled away for ages until one morning, over breakfast, it exploded. We were playing away and therefore had spent the night in a hotel. I was sitting at a table with Chris Lawler and Tommy, who ordered his full English, and then sat there, impatience building, waiting for his order to arrive.

Fifteen minutes later, Emlyn rushed in, late on parade. As he sat down, the waiter bustled by with Tommy's breakfast. 'I'll have that!' called out Emlyn.

The waiter obliged and put the food in front of a hungry Emlyn, whereupon he duly tucked into the eggs and bacon.

Well, fuck me! All hell broke loose. Bread rolls went flying. Condiments crashed and clashed. I swear to God, I thought Tommy was going to batter Emlyn – who just kept on eating!

'Order another one,' says Emlyn. 'Hey! Waiter! Bring another breakfast over here for my mate. The man's starving.'

So, poor old Tommy had to wait another 15 minutes for his breakfast. That episode did nothing to ease tension between these two giants, but it was like water off a duck's back for Emlyn, because that's how he was.

But the fact that they were at war could be bloody tough for me at times. I remember a particular match when we were playing Swansea, and they were absolutely NOT on speaking terms. In this particular game, Emlyn was playing at left-back, Tommy on the right and I was in the middle. How I managed to play the match with the dialogue going on either side of me was nothing short of a miracle. Emlyn, who was aware that weight was an issue for the older man, would yell to me, 'Tell that fat bastard to move out faster!'

Then Tommy would call across, 'Tell that big-headed bastard to move the ball forward quicker and not pose on it for so fucking long!'

It was nuts – especially as I wasn't the best character to be a mediator.

In his first few matches for Liverpool, Emlyn's energy far outweighed his skill. His wild charges up field, with tackles resembling illegal throws in Cumberland wrestling, earned him the nickname 'Crazy Horse'. Thankfully he settled down.

If Kevin Keegan was the most talented of our players, Emlyn wasn't far behind. He was a loveable character with his high voice and cheeky face, and hugely popular with players (except with Tommy Smith of course), management and the Kopites. You just sensed that Liverpool was almost as much a part of his life as it was Bill Shankly's, and this is probably the reason, more than anything else, why the two of them hit it off so well.

Emlyn loved to tell the story about when Shanks was signing him. They had to go to Lytham St Anne's to complete the signing, so that Emlyn could play straight away in Liverpool's very next match. Well, according to Emlyn, the ten-minute journey was a bit hair-raising to say the least.

He was a terrible driver, according to Emlyn. He had this old brown Corsair, and they hadn't got far from the ground when they came to a set of traffic lights. At first Shanks wasn't going to stop, but suddenly he changed his mind, slammed on the brakes and skidded to a halt.

The woman behind shunted straight into the back of them and there was the sound of breaking glass as headlights were smashed. Shanks and the woman got out of their cars, exchanged numbers and they went on their way. Suddenly blue lights were flashing and a police car pulled them over. A young copper got out, sauntered over to the car and gestured for Shanks to wind the window down, which he did.

'What is it, officer?' asks Shanks innocently.

'I'm sorry, sir, but I can't let you drive this car. You've got no lights. It's illegal.'

Shanks explained what had just happened but it was no good. The copper insisted they had to get the car fixed before driving it any further.

Then Shanks flew into action. 'Don't you realise who is in this car?'

Emlyn thought, 'How embarrassing – he's going to do the "Don't you realise who I am?" routine.'

But he didn't. Instead, he poked his head through the open window and in his broad Scottish accent he growled, 'No, not me, you fool, I just happen to have the future captain of England alongside me.'

They had a very special relationship, Shanks and Emlyn. I guess they were very similar in some ways. Both had this incredible work ethic, and they shared the same passion for Liverpool – I swear Emlyn hated the colour blue as much as Shanks did. I think if Shanks ever *did* have a favourite player it would be Emlyn, and that favouritism would have been born out of these similarities in character.

Emlyn was dynamite during the seventies and I have no doubt that Shanks looked upon Emlyn as being head of the new guard. This didn't endear him to the old guard who remained loyal to Tommy. As I said before, it was an era of clans!

I was deeply saddened when Emlyn died prematurely at the age of just 57. Emlyn, Tommy Smith and I had forged great partnerships on the pitch and, although Tommy and Emlyn clashed, I regarded both of them, individually, as good pals.

Ray Clemence was my best pal, though. We used to go everywhere together. But I have to say, he let me down badly on one occasion. Us newcomers wanted more money. By now we were earning £120 a week. We felt it was far too low and, compared to the wages of professional footballers today, it was a mere pittance. 'Let's stick together when we ask for a rise' was the agreement, as this would mean being in a position of power. Off us boys went to see the club secretary, Peter Robinson, and put in a request for an improved pay packet. One hundred and eighty pounds per week was the sum we'd agreed on, but all the club would offer was £150.

You can imagine what a complete jerk I looked when, as I was standing in front of Peter Robinson giving it large about how us lads were sticking to our guns, he looked up and said, 'Ray actually signed two weeks ago for £150.'

My mate had caved in. I was gutted, as I was certain if we'd held out we would have got the higher sum. You know, Sue and I didn't want the extra money for a fucking Ferrari or a palatial home; we just wanted to be able to buy some baby clothes for our new baby boy (Damian) who was on the way, and a dolly's pram for Yolanda!

The changes at Anfield just kept on coming. If the team of the late sixties didn't know it initially, by the start of the 1970/71 season they were left in no doubt. The season started well and kept on going well. Although I was still fighting to establish myself in the Liverpool team, I consider this to have been one of my best seasons with them. Having played the six final games of the previous season in the first team, and being told I was to be first-choice centre-half for the start of the next, boosted my confidence no end.

It's amazing the difference it makes when you are told you are good at something. It seems to up your performance. The man-management from Shankly and his sidekick Bob Paisley was quite something. They forewarned me that I would have some indifferent games, but I was not to worry, as this was simply because of my age and lack of experience. But, they added with encouragement, that I wouldn't be dropped because of a bad performance or two.

They were convinced that I had the ability to make the No.5 shirt my own and were prepared to stand by me and back their initial judgement. When you are told something like that, it immediately lifts a lot of pressure from your shoulders, and in my mind's eye that is brilliant management.

Only Ian Callaghan, Tommy Smith and Chris Lawler from the old guard could now consider themselves regulars in the big team. Although we weren't expected to win the league, Liverpool Football Club demanded that, despite all the changes, we *must* finish in the top six, and qualify for Europe – and we did it. There were hiccups on the way, but what mattered in the end was that we made the grade.

In fact, there was a massive achievement just around the corner. There was also a disappointment; but, hey, you can't have it all.

CHAPTER 10

THE 1971 FA CUP FINAL –
LIVERPOOL V ARSENAL

MY FIRST FULL season in the Liverpool side saw us finishing third in the league and reaching the FA Cup final at Wembley. Getting to Wembley in my first season as a regular seemed unbelievable – but it was true.

I remember the whole experience so clearly. The day we left for London's Wembley, a new and exciting young boy – namely Kevin Keegan – signed for us. Little did we know that this little man sitting on a dustbin waving us off with his girlfriend was to turn into a phenomenal player and huge football celebrity.

You don't need me to tell you about Kevin Keegan and the massive career he went on to have. But I'll tell you this much, he worked like a Trojan. I personally don't think he possessed a natural talent, but, shit, he gave his all. As far as the media were concerned, with his good looks and curly locks, he was the Beckham of our day. Most players have to spend a short spell in the reserves, but not Keegan – he zoomed straight into playing with the big boys. I guess

81

it was a shame we couldn't play him in this FA Cup final —maybe he might just have made all the difference to the outcome.

The mood on the team coach as we travelled south was charged with such electricity, such a sense of anticipation, that it was difficult to contain my excitement. This was a feeling that I'd waited all my young life to experience.

I had already supplied the match tickets for my family, but, unbeknown to me, ITV's popular broadcaster Brian Moore arranged transport for my family to go to Wembley.

Along with the club directors, my team-mates and I were whiling away the day at Hendon Hall hotel watching the build-up on the television when Brian Moore's voice announced, 'The Celebrity Bus is here.'

Everyone sat up and took more notice, wondering who was arriving. Was it royalty? Perhaps it was a pop star or an actor?

From the distance, an old bus rattled to the forefront of the screen and stopped next to Brian Moore.

The bus, which was probably used by social services in its heyday, turned out to be a spot-on mode of transport for the passengers who were just beginning to alight. The special Cup final day celebrities only turned out to be my family. I nearly died with embarrassment when my lovely old mum, all five-foot-nothing of her, jumped from the bottom step, landed next to Brian Moore and grinned into the camera as he thrust the mike in her flushed face.

'Good afternoon, Mrs Lloyd, tell us, are you proud of your son?'

To my horror, my mum decided to go posh and it went terribly wrong as she managed to get all her 'h's in the wrong place. 'Yes, ee his the pride of Bristol. We har 'avin a lovely day hout thanks to Hi TV.'

Oh, good God — let the ground open up and swallow me!

But there was much worse to come. Quickly following Mum off

the bus was my oldest brother Barney who began, in a thick West Country accent, to moan into the microphone. 'Ee's [Ivan] got bleeding cramp from being cooped up on that there looney bus.'

Please tell me this isn't happening!

Later, my mum told me they had been behaving very badly all the way down the M4, hanging out the windows drooling and pretending to be... well, how can I put this? Not the full shilling. My family – can't take 'em anywhere!

Next to devastate me was my brother Fuzz and his wife, Margaret, who for some reason that I never quite worked out, as it was a sweltering hot day, were dressed in matching thick Aran sweaters.

Our Marj, having dealt with the press many times before, decided she wanted to be interviewer instead of interviewee and tried to grab the microphone from poor old Brian Moore who didn't know what the hell was happening to him! The spectacle of my big sister struggling for supremacy was actually pretty funny – although at the time I was having a sense-of-humour bypass!

Next off the bus was my brother Ivan, who, when asked about his brother Larry, yelled, 'I be a better footballer than eee.'

Finally, bringing up the rear were my last two brothers Jake and Bert, who had clearly been boozing on the bus and stumbled down the steps asking, 'Where's bleedin ale then?'

All this time we were watching this spectacle back at Hendon Hall, and I was sinking lower and lower into my chair, bright red with embarrassment. But, on reflection, after all these years, the Liverpool lads taking the piss out of me seemed to ease the pre-match tension.

But the excitement was growing with every passing moment, and finally it was time to line up in the tunnel. I get a shiver up and down every time I recall this experience.

When I walked through that tunnel and out on to the Wembley turf with the mighty Liverpool who were about to clash with the equally mighty Arsenal, it was a complete dream come true.

The atmosphere was like nothing I had ever known. It had been mental enough when I first walked out at a home fixture at Anfield to the screams of almost 60,000 fans, which had been some contrast to the lowly 5,000 at Bristol. But this Wembley experience, with a 100,000 attendance, surpassed everything.

I could see my 'looney' family standing on the seats waving frantically to me from the stand – my mum, my brothers, sister, but alas not my dad. I had a thought that I hoped he was looking down on me with pride.

We played well, but Arsenal were the better side that day in that they played with sheer guts and determination. There were no goals in regular time, although George Graham came close with a header that hit the crossbar with 12 minutes to go – that made our hearts stop! Just two minutes into extra time, Steve Heighway managed to sneak a ball past Bob Wilson, but what was seen to be a mistake by Wilson was counteracted when Eddie Kelly levelled for the Gunners nine minutes later.

But devastation happened for us in the shape of the long-haired Charlie George who let fly with a cracking 20-yard shot which Ray Clemence didn't have a hope in hell of saving.

You can imagine the crushing disappointment when we lost to them. I will never forget the sight of Charlie George lying on the pitch in celebration after scoring the winning goal. We were all in tears, and at a moment like that you feel as if you are never going to recover.

Arsenal were happy though. They did the double that year. But it could have been us doing the double and, oh boy, I was gutted. It's quite amazing how one can go through so many different emotions in one day.

I think the thought that helped me through the following 24 hours was that I knew I was with a team who would be back to win trophies, and soon.

As for Bill Shankly. I don't think I ever saw him as upset as he was right then. When we lost this FA Cup final, his face was wracked with disappointment. I knew then that his bark was worse than his bite, and this oft-menacing character had a soft spot buried inside.

Still, there was always next season. We went off for a summer break and tried to forget about the disappointment.

IN NEED OF A HOLIDAY

There were so many pre-season and post-season holidays, and not all were with our other halves. Some of them were 'lads-only' jolly-ups. Sue would never believe this – not till this day – but I always missed her terribly on these occasions. The break that sticks mostly in my mind was the one we were given by the Liverpool directors as a reward for reaching the FA Cup final and finishing third in the league. We went off to our favourite resort in Majorca. It was a real boozy affair.

After being on a bender for much of the day, we grabbed a quick shower to freshen up, before resuming our drinking marathon. Before leaving my room to join the rest of the lads, I decided to ring home to speak to Sue and see how my eight-month-old daughter Yolanda was.

On hearing my baby girl say 'Dada' down the phone, I became morose. I was missing my girls like mad. I shouldn't have gone out drinking again, but, hey, I was a footballer, and this was supposed to be a full-on 'boys behaving badly' time! So I went out and took my morose head with me.

Later, and absolutely steaming, we all fell into a nightclub. I needed the toilet, but, being a bit of a lunatic in those days, I decided to barge my way through the packed dance floor, elbowing people out of the way as I went. Halfway across, I stumbled, knocked a drink out of some poor bloke's hand and, with no word of an apology, staggered onwards towards the gents. I felt this blow on the back of my head – the result of a mighty punch. I turned and blindly threw a punch at the nearest guy, and within seconds was surrounded by bouncers armed with baseball bats, all threatening to break them over my head if I didn't leave. I went. It's amazing how you sober up at the sight of baseball bats hovering over your head.

The following evening, I had the audacity to return to the club, but, if I'm honest, I really wanted to say sorry to the bloke I'd punched. It wasn't like me to cause trouble, and it made me realise just how dangerous booze can be when you are feeling low. As I stood by the bar waiting for a glimpse of my victim, I got a tap on the shoulder and there he stood, sporting a black eye. The poor bloke told me how confused he'd been to get a left hook from a stranger for no good reason. He hadn't been the guy who had punched me – he had been an innocent bystander. After my profuse apologies, we had a few pints together and ended up good pals.

But I'd learned a lesson. Don't drink when you're on a downer. It's a shame I forgot this golden rule many years later when my life hit a crisis point. The memory bank can bloody well let you down when you're drunk.

CHAPTER 11

PLAYING FOR
ENGLAND

IN 1971, MUCH to my delight, I was selected to represent England in
the Under 23s in a match against West Germany. My team-mates Ray
Clemence and Alun Evans were also chosen, which was a bonus as it's
always good to share special occasions with people you know well.

What first struck me when I met Sir Alf Ramsey was how
different he was as a manager to 'Brimstone and Fire' Shankly. His
style was very, very different. Alf used a quiet methodical approach
and, to be honest, I found it really pleasant. I liked him a lot. While
Middlesbrough's Harold Shepperdson led the training sessions, Alf
would move around the squad having a quiet word in your ear now
and again. Nothing was made complicated and there were no
histrionics. He kept everything simple. 'I've watched you play on
several occasions for Liverpool, Larry, and I want you to play in
exactly the same way for England.'

So I did. We won 3–1 and I played well. After the game Alf was
the same dignified gentleman, not demonstrative at all. He

congratulated us all collectively and then went on to have quiet individual words with his players.

He stroked his chin as he said to me, 'There was one incident out there that I'm not sure about.'

I shrugged in confusion.

'It was in the second half, Larry. The German centre-forward received the ball wide on the right. You moved in to tackle him and he tried to pass you on the outside. Remember?'

I certainly did remember. I remembered that he pushed the ball a little too far ahead of him, and that gave me the opportunity to make my tackle. A hard crunching tackle if I remembered right! It was so hard that both the ball and the player finished up flying over a small wall surrounding the running track.

I couldn't see Sir Alf's problem. The referee had deemed it a 'legal' tackle.

'You asked me to play how I play for Liverpool, and that's how I play for my club,' I said.

At that point, an FA official broke up our one-to-one, and Alf walked away from me. But a few yards away he looked over his shoulder and winked at me. I surmised I should keep on playing in this fashion. What he had just done was to do his duty by bringing it to my attention that this really wasn't the best behaviour for good relationships between England and Germany. 'A bit late for that,' I thought. I didn't give a fuck!

I had played a couple of other England Under-23 matches, and like all young ambitious footballers I was praying I'd get the chance to play in the full team – and sooner rather than later. I was already in the squad and, when we were flying back from France, something very special happened to me. Sir Alf came and sat beside me. I gulped in surprise, 'Hello, Alf!'

'Larry, I have a great favour to ask of you. There is an Under-23 team tour of Eastern Europe coming up, and I need a centre-half. How are you fixed?'

How was I fixed?

'Can you help me out?'

Could I help him out? You bet!

Here I was, returning from a full England match and the manager asked me if I'd like to go home and spend a few days with my family before joining him and the rest of the squad in London. He told me that as I had been away on tour I could take a break and, instead of beginning pre-match training at the weekend with the rest of the lads, I could join them on the Tuesday.

It was approaching midday when I checked into the Whites Hotel. The players had already gone to the training ground in Roehampton, so I jumped in a taxi and went off to join the squad.

Sir Alf strolled over to me. 'Thanks for coming, Larry.' (*He* was thanking *me*!!) 'But it seems we have a slight problem here.'

'Oh, shit!' I thought. 'What the fuck's coming next?'

'Several weeks ago, the players were all measured for suits for the tour. Obviously you weren't there. What I suggest is… Do you know London well?'

'No,' I gulped. 'Not at all, really.'

'OK, what I suggest is this. No need for you to join in training. Get yourself into a taxi, and go over to Oxford Street and buy yourself a dark-blue suit.' He took £500 from his pocket and handed it to me.

Now, this was one hell of a lump of money in the seventies and I was well chuffed. So I toddled off to the heart of London and pulled myself a lovely dark-blue suit off the peg. It was really smart, and turned out to be much more fashionable than the suits my team-mates had got, so I got a bit of stick! It only cost £350 as well, so I got more than one result.

When I got back to the hotel I showered and then got the lift to go for dinner. It just so happened that Sir Alf was also in the lift.

He turned to me. 'Did you get your suit?'

'Yes, thanks.'

'Well…' He cleared his throat and, in his posh voice, said, 'I have another favour to ask you.'

Crikey. Another favour. It struck me I was bending over backwards for Sir Alf.

'How would you like to captain my England Under-23 side?'

Now it was my turn to clear *my* throat! 'Thank you very much, sir,' is all I managed to say. Unbelievable. How many people have been asked that particular favour? Not too many. I felt so honoured.

I went to join the others for a pre-dinner drink. I'd been told not to tell them yet. Sir Alf wanted to break the news at an official meeting. I noticed they had set up a gambling book, taking odds on who was going to be asked to be captain. 'What's happening, boys?' I asked, and then, when I was told about the bet, I added, 'Oh, I don't suppose I'm in the running?'

'Nah, I'll give you 10 to 1.' I can't remember whether it was Kevin Keegan, Ray Clemence or Malcolm McDonald, who joked about this.

Then Sir Alf summoned us to the meeting and announced, 'I've invited Larry to be captain, and he has accepted.'

You should have seen their faces! I think a few said, 'Fuck you, Lloydie.'

But, as I said to them, I could have made a fortune if I'd bet on myself. 'Look, I saved you money,' I said, grinning.

I remember that time as clear as if it was yesterday.

I can't tell you how chuffed I was being invited to be captain. It was truly one of my proudest moments. After playing over in Europe on the tour, we returned to my home town of Bristol where we played West Germany. My mum and some of my brothers came to watch. They didn't need a bus this time, thank God!

When I think about that tour, I recall two particular stories which make me laugh out loud.

The first tale is about my friend Frank Worthington's team-mate Alan Birchenall at Leicester, and the second about Mad Frankie himself.

In one of the matches, Alan was awarded 'Man of the Match' for his outstanding movement around the pitch. Some time later, I got to know this incredible striker well, and he explained to me why his lightning movement was so outstanding and had been likened to Disney's Roadrunner character.

'Larry,' he said, grinning, 'I was running away from you and Tommy Smith. You were tough bastards and, fuck me, you could kick! You two fucking bastards were kicking me to death. I decided to save myself by running out wide and leave dopy Worthington to take the kickings.'

The reason Frank came to get a call up to the tour was because we lost Malcolm Macdonald with a bad knee injury during our game against East Germany and he had to go home. Sir Alf chose my old mate centre-forward Frank Worthington to be his replacement, and we had arranged to meet him at Warsaw airport.

Now, Alf obviously knew what a great footballer Frank was, but, unlike yours truly, he knew nothing of his crazy personality. 'Larry,' said Alf, 'we must keep a lookout for Frank Worthington.'

Frank Worthington was Elvis crazy and, as we waited patiently in arrivals, suddenly, in the distance, the tall, slim Frank came into view

– a Frank who really rated his looks. He thought he was good-looking but I guess it was a matter of opinion.

On his head sat a cowboy hat and he had this string-tie thing hanging round his neck. The tightest-fitting jeans I had ever seen and a pair of cowboy boots finished off the effect. He looked absolutely hysterical. It was a case of *Worthington is dead and Elvis lives*.

He swaggered closer and closer, and as he reached our sides I turned to the boss and introduced him. 'Sir Alf Ramsey, this is Frank Worthington.'

Sir Alf's jaw dropped to his chest. In a posh accent that sounded very strange indeed, he said, 'Oh, fuck… I hope you have a proper shirt with you?' Sir Alf had sworn! A very rare occurrence, I can tell you.

Let me tell you another quickie about Frank. I remember once, when Liverpool were playing Leicester and we defeated them heavily in a one-sided 5–0 victory, their manager, Jimmy Bloomfield, blew a gasket. He was giving his team a right bollocking. 'Where the fuck's Frank?' (Jimmy wasn't as posh as Sir Alf.)

Frank was happily singing his favourite Elvis hit 'Blue Suede Shoes' in the shower at the top of his voice. 'One for the money… two for the…'

Jimmy leaped into action and I'll leave the rest to your imagination. Oh, the air was bluer than those blue suede shoes.

While at Leicester City, he allegedly caught the eye of young hopeful Gary Lineker. Then he played for Bolton Wanderers before he took his flamboyant and outrageous character to Elland Road, where, although he didn't actually play for them for very long, he became a Leeds United legend.

The reason I'm telling you so much about Frank is because, like me, he is always prepared to speak his mind, and he has strong views about what he called 'greedy superstar footballers' of our modern game. Like me, he too believes some managers today stifle the gifted boys who have a natural flair. Frank, like Georgie Best, played in the streets around his home.

That wasn't the only thing he had in common with Bestie. He liked to bed a good-looking woman and is proud to admit that he has lived a sex, drink, drugs and rock'n'roll lifestyle. I can't say I shared that particular lifestyle however!

People often ask me about Alf Ramsey. Was this posh England manager, who had been knighted in 1967, a hero or a villain? In my book he's a hero for his 1966 World Cup triumph. But, as always, it's a matter of opinion. Personally, I liked the man, and responded well to his gentlemanly manner.

I have heard some call him humourless and a bore, full of negativity. But, as you have just heard, I have first-hand experience of his humour. His critics used to say that he was aloof and proud, but I think he got his priorities right. I liked it that he allowed us to simply call him Alf. So there were no airs and graces in that department.

You wouldn't have known it, but he actually came from a working-class background. He disliked bad manners and seriously disliked the media. He's not alone there.

Before becoming the England manager, he had enjoyed a successful career playing for Tottenham Hotspur. In 1948 he made his England debut against Switzerland, and he earned three caps. On the pitch, he was cool, calm and collected – just as he was off it. Well known for his coolness in taking penalties, he earned the nickname 'The General of Penalties'. There was no way he could possibly be described as a quick nippy player. Instead, he moved slowly but purposefully around the pitch with great poise, awareness and strength. He also read the game well, which was one of the reasons he was a good manager.

You could say that he was the first 'real' English manager we had ever had, as, when he took over in 1963, he demanded total control over squad selections. Before Ramsey, committee members had made such decisions.

I found him strict but fair, and I think this typifies him as a manager. He always kept you on your toes, always left you wondering whether you were going to get your place in the team, making you work hard and really focus.

It was said that he liked to play thuggish defenders, best typified by Norbert 'Nobby' Stiles and Norman 'Bites Your Legs' Hunter; luckily for Larry 'Brick Wall' Lloyd, this is true.

Yes, there were lots of 1–0 scores, and some were boringly defensive, but 1–0 at the end of the day is a win. And at the end of the day he had the best win of all – the 1966 World Cup. When he took on the England managerial job, he boldly predicted England would win the next World Cup. How's that for positive visualisation!

He had very little success with England throughout the seventies, and he was sacked in 1974 after England failed to qualify for the World Cup tournament that year.

He suffered from the terrible Alzheimer's disease for quite some time, before he died in a nursing home in 1999, at the age of 79. The tributes rolled in. Sir Bobby Charlton was shocked and said, 'I couldn't be more upset if it was a member of my family.'

And Tony Blair commented, 'Sir Alf Ramsey gave England the greatest moment in sporting history.'

As for me, I liked the man. I just wished I could have earned more England caps. I played in the Under 23s eight times and then earned four full international caps. I just wished I could have earned more. That said, I'm very proud of the ones I got.

Let me tell you about them. It wasn't exactly a long and illustrious England career, but it was certainly eventful!

CHAPTER 12

ENGLAND FULL CAPS

ENGLAND v WALES, Home Championship, 19 May 1971
Attendance: 70,000

As well as it being my debut match for the full team, Tommy Smith and West Brom's Tony Brown were also called up to play their first matches for their country. Sir Alf Ramsey was perhaps risking his reputation by making such radical changes to his team, but it was a chance he was obviously willing to take. He had already shown his willingness to take a chance on me, and now I was about to win my first cap.

This was the second of three Home Championship matches. A few days before we had played Northern Ireland and won 1–0. Our critics had said we were lucky to get the win, and that the Irish had shown far more flair than us. Certainly, had it not been for Gordon Banks playing out of his skin and keeping a clean sheet they would have beaten us. But that's football – a win is a win. Now we were hoping for another victory, and nobody was more excited than me, a boy barely in his twenties.

The team on this spring day at Wembley consisted of the legendary Peter Shilton in goal, Manchester City's Francis Lee in the middle of the field, West Brom's Tony Brown (later substituted by Leeds' Alan Clarke) and Spurs player Ralph Coates. Then there were West Ham United and 1966 World Cup heroes Geoff Hurst and Martin Peters, the latter being our skipper. The Liverpool fans must have been really proud that four of their players — namely Chris Lawler, Emlyn Hughes, Tommy Smith and yours truly — were out there playing for Queen and country.

I'd like to say I got off to a brilliant flying start, but the truth was I nearly scored a bloody own goal! Peter Shilton and I did this sort of demented dance around each other and thank fuck he managed to get his arms around my frantic, wild clearance or my first cap would probably have been my last! I don't know if it was nerves or down to my eagerness to defend my country; all I know is that I nearly died on the spot and I had to raise my game pretty sharpish. Let's call it teething troubles, shall we?

Then, within seconds, the other new boy, striker Tony Brown, crossed a tidy header that almost saw him score — at the right end — and you could say we both quickly learned what top-flight English football was all about. The only difference being he would have been a hero and I'd have been the villain!

Wales had John Toshack on their side. He was on brilliant form, as was Terry Yorath, so the teams were a good match. Francis Lee did manage to score but it was ruled offside because good old Tony Brown was standing in an offside position. Soon after, Martin Peters shot a cracker on target but the Welsh goalkeeper Gary Sprake (Leeds United) caught the ball and held it close to him for all his life was worth.

During the second half Sir Alf pulled off Tony Brown and

replaced him with Alan Clarke. I think he was looking for some maturity and to inject some life up front, which was a good move as within minutes he'd almost scored; but almost is no good, and it ended up a miserable goalless draw, which was, in some ways, an anti-climax for me and the other new boys. But I wouldn't have missed the experience for the world.

Our reviews were mixed, with some saying we were really unlucky not to win, while others reckoned we were disorganised and a bit chaotic. One report said we were 'lacklustre in attack and didn't show enough authority in defence'. They also said we missed Bobby Moore badly and I guess we did, as he wasn't a bad player in his time! Just kidding, you Hammers. In all seriousness, I do believe Martin Peters and Geoff Hurst *did* miss old Mooro, and, on a personal note, I was pissed off he wasn't playing too – but later in the year I would get to play alongside him.

ENGLAND v SWITZERLAND, European Qualifier, 10 November
Attendance: 98,000

It was six months later that I got my next call-up. Again, the match was played at home at Wembley, and again it ended in a draw – this time 1–1. It was our tenth match of all time against Switzerland, who were a young team but nevertheless played lovely, attractive football (a bit like me!). Their immaturity as a side began to show in the second half when they began to tire, though, and we went one up after Mike Summerbee looped a header over the Swiss goalkeeper. Now we were in the driving seat, up and running and looking likely winners. I was out there on the pitch with two World Cup heroes – Alan Ball, who was at Everton at that time, and West Ham's Bobby Moore. I was playing with Mooro at last!

Instead of the Swiss dropping off in their performance after our goal, they upped their game and got stuck in. On 26 minutes, they equalised – and, I have to say, the goal was outstanding, their attacker Odermatt firing a terrific shot from at least 25 yards out. Shilts didn't stand a chance of saving it; I think he got his fingers to it, but it was too fierce and too fast.

We were aware of the noisy home crowd chanting Rodney Marsh's name. The fans were clearly not happy about Rodders being on the bench. Finally, and I don't know whether this was due to pressure from the terraces or because Sir Alf had made up his own mind up, whatever, on came the Queens Park Rangers forward and off went a dejected Francis Lee.

I was disappointed we could only manage a draw again. I desperately wanted us to win. But it could have been worse. Had it not been for the best goalie England has ever seen (in my humble opinion) saving yet another belter from Odermatt – this time bending a free-kick over the cross-bar – we would have lost, and that really would have sent me to the bar afterwards to drown my sorrows.

The only good thing was that England managed to retain the lead in our group table. Only a defeat in our next match against Greece by four or more goals would see us fail to gain a place in the quarter-finals of the European Qualifier Championships.

Derby's Roy McFarland, who was the regular England centre-half, was back in the side so I wasn't selected to play in Pireus, which was a bastard as we won 2–0 and I would have finally been involved in a triumphant match for my country. It was no pushover of a match as the second goal didn't come until the final minute of normal time, but the lads won, and that was all that mattered.

ENGLAND v WEST GERMANY, European Nations' Cup
quarter-final, first leg, 29 April 1972
Attendance: 95,000

During the build-up to this monumental match, I was Sir Alf Ramsey's understudy to Roy McFarland. When Roy was sent home from training camp with an injury, I was convinced I was the natural replacement. To be honest, so did everyone else in the squad, as did the press who had me named in the starting line-up.

During the training session the day before the biggest match England had played in years, I played like a dream. I was hyped up and adrenalin was coursing through my veins. In my mind, this was to be my biggest international to date by far.

At the end of training, Sir Alf took us to the far end of the ground, away from the prying eyes and ears of the paparazzi, and in the spring sunshine told us to sit on the grass. He then began his task of telling us the team in the starting line-up, beginning with the goalkeeper Gordon Banks. Then he called out Emlyn Hughes's name, followed by Colin Bell. I sat up straighter as he came to the names of the two central defenders. Then I heard him say, 'Bobby Moore and Norman Hunter.'

I couldn't quite comprehend what was happening and, to be honest, nor could the other squad members. I didn't hear any more names clearly. I had been expecting my name next – and so had everyone else. All eyes were on me as I tried to digest the fact that Norman was in and not me. I must have looked a sorry sight down there on the grass with my head in my hands close to tears. I don't think I'd ever felt such a disappointment. I was absolutely gutted. I couldn't fathom it. Norman played the same position for Leeds as Bobby played for West Ham, which was playing alongside a big burly centre-half – like me. Of course I could understand Bobby's selection – but Norman and not me? I barely heard the other names of Francis Lee, Alan Ball, Martin Chivers, Geoff Hurst and Martin Peters and I never got a wink of sleep that night.

The match was watched by noisy and excitable fans from England and Germany, and had anyone in the stands been neutral they would have enjoyed a thoroughly entertaining match with four goals worthy of a match of this magnitude. I honestly can't emphasise enough how much hype there had been in the media about old enemies England and Germany locking horns at Wembley. It was even dubbed the 'Match of the Century'.

But I'll tell you something, sitting there on the bench watching the wizardry of the Germans was something else. Beckenbauer was pure magic, and midfielders Netzer, Hoeness and Wimmer were on fire, with Grabowski and Held fast and furious out on the wings. When I say we were so slow we were almost going backwards I am neither exaggerating nor is it a case of sour grapes; we were hesitant and indecisive. Even hero Bobby Moore – who quite literally never put a foot wrong – made an error which led to the German's first goal. He was trying to dribble the ball clear of our penalty area, but Hoeness nicked the ball off him and hit – I think – a deflected shot into the net. My head went back down and I was even more frustrated I couldn't get out there and be part of the action. Sitting on the bench is never pleasant but when it's the alleged match of the century… well, I'm lost for words.

The lads tried and tried. They played their hearts out, constantly pushing forward, only to have all attempts on goal saved by the terrific German goalie Maier. We were outplayed in midfield, which is astonishing, given that we had Alan Ball, Martin Peters and Colin Bell playing their hearts out. But we were missing Alan Mullery's flair, and I'm certain that's what made the difference.

The first half ended with us that one goal down. We came out for the second half firing on all cylinders but simply could not find a way through their strong defensive line-up, until, finally, we broke through and 15 minutes before the end of the match the lads won their equaliser. The build-up began with Martin Peters and Colin Bell out on the right wing. Colin had a good shot on goal that moved my arse off the bench ready to cheer. He missed – damn – then Frannie Lee, quick as a flash, got a foot to the ball and in the baby went. Bench or no bench, I couldn't have been more delighted.

The last six minutes were a nightmare. I don't like to single out any player as being extra bad but poor old Bobby Moore was definitely off colour. He was outpaced by Held, and in a dodgy tackle Held went down and the Germans were given a penalty that went in off the post. Were they lucky to get awarded the penalty? From where I was sitting on a hard wooden bastard bench, I'd say they were, but there didn't seem to be much luck going on at all in my department.

Minutes later Muller spun more magic and pulled their third goal out of a clever reverse pass by Hoeness and it was all over.

As for me, there was one small consolation. Two big companies, Adidas and Puma, had supplied football boots to the selected team members, of which I had been one (I told you everyone thought I'd be playing). All the other players had sponsorship deals with one or the other and were therefore paid by just one company. I, on the other hand, had no deals so I could have chosen which pair to wear. Both had already given me the sponsorship money upfront – so I sat for 90 minutes with an Adidas boot on my left foot and a Puma on my right. So you see, there is some truth in every cloud having a silver lining!

ENGLAND v NORTHERN IRELAND, 23 May 1972,
Home Championship
Attendance: 43,000

We lost 1–0 and I was gutted. I had felt sure I was going to be involved in a winning match at last, as Northern Ireland had not beaten us in Wembley Stadium since 1957 – when I had been a nine-year-old just beginning to enjoy a game of football. Surely it was a dead cert? Nope.

Of course, the Irish fans in the crowd went wild when they scored. We went wild as well, but there was no happiness to be found in our wildness. Our 'wild' was of the angry variety – angry with ourselves for conceding. Their goal scorer, Terry Neill, who played for Hull City and was celebrating his 51st cap for his country, slammed the ball home at close range.

We tried so hard to come back at them but their defence was solid as a rock. I have to give it to the Irish, though, they really did deserve this glorious win.

Little did I know my England career was to be cut short, and it was doubly upsetting as it was due to a mixture of events rather than me not being good enough.

I was picked to play for England again soon after this defeat at the hands of the Irish, but, due to club commitments with Liverpool (we had a League Cup replay), I had to decline the offer. Naturally, I thought I was in for a good shout of being picked again, but a change of management put paid to that. Don Revie, who had worked wonders with Leeds United by taking them from a mediocre side to one of the most consistent in the country, had made him the FA's obvious choice to take over from Sir Alf Ramsey in 1974. I guess Don didn't fancy me in his side, and it didn't help that soon afterwards Liverpool sold me to Coventry; once I was there, everything, including my fitness (due to injuries), went rapidly downhill.

I was upset and angry but I only really had myself to blame. If I had hung on in at Liverpool, I think I would have earned more caps during the seventies; in fact, I'm certain of it.

It wasn't until several years down the line, when Cloughie had elevated me back to the top of the game, that I was selected again – but I'll tell you all about that after I've taken you back to more stories, both on and off the pitch, at Liverpool and Coventry – and the wonderful Nottingham Forest.

CHAPTER 13

TRIUMPHANT LIVERPOOL

FIRST LEG OF UEFA CUP – Anfield, 10 May 1973
Back in 1965, Shankly's team came agonisingly close to being the first British team to make it to the European Cup final. Unfortunately, they were controversially knocked out by Inter Milan in the semi-finals.

The following year, they reached the Cup Winners Cup final only to lose to West Germany's Borussia Dortmund when Ron Yeats scored an own goal. European success eluded the club until 1973 when our Liverpool side beat Borussia Monchengladbach 3–2 on aggregate in the UEFA Cup final. It was something very special.

THE RAIN WAS torrential and half an hour into the first leg of the first round the referee took the only decision he could – to abandon play. The pitch by now resembled a lake. The ever astute Shanks had seen enough of the German side's problems in the air and by the time we came out to play the game the following day he had brought John Toshack into the side. It was John who set up Kevin Keegan with two goals in the first half.

I can remember lining up in the tunnel at Anfield. I thought back to how I felt in my first game as a professional at Bristol Rovers. Then my memory flitted on to my debut game for Liverpool, and finally to my debut at Anfield. It was like a reel of cinematography clicking away in my brain. Soon I was to have another wonderful snapshot to tuck away in my memory, because I only bloody scored the third goal in that first brilliant half. How about that!

There could have been two more goals during that 45 minutes, but Kevin missed a penalty and then Josef Heynckes was awarded a penalty that Ray Clemence thankfully managed to save. It finished 3–0 – it was yours truly that scored the winning goal. Can I say that again? I scored the bloody winning goal!

When I was with Bristol Rovers and scored a miraculous goal I was over the moon, but this was an out-of-body experience. I am not a goal scorer – I play at the back and defend. That's what I do. So when I headed one home in the UEFA Cup I nearly died on the spot. I've never known anything like it and doubt I ever will again. But that once-in-a-lifetime moment is good enough for me. If I could have changed anything about that goal, it would have been to score it at the Liverpool supporters' end.

I headed the ball into the net from Keegan's corner. Oh, I jumped and hugged and if I could have sprinted to the other end to leap about with those fabulous Liverpool supporters I would have – but I was a big fucker and could leg it nowhere!

There were 55,000 of our fans chanting and, not many minutes later, the whistle blew and it was game over. As someone who has been dubbed the most underestimated player of his time, I think of this mind-blowing moment with pride. Shit, I was fucking good that day.

TRIUMPHANT LIVERPOOL

*SECOND LEG UEFA CUP FINAL – Borussia-Park,
Monchengladbach, 23 May 1973*

Taking a three-goal lead to the German side was a great advantage
and, as it turned out, much needed – especially the one I'd scored,
of course.

Shankly played the same team as the first leg, and we were all
happy about that as we were gelling well. But despite all this we
were two goals down by half-time. In our team talk during the
break Shanks told us to keep our heads and go out and play as he
knew we could and we'd win the UEFA Cup. We did as the boss
said, and as the second half progressed they became tired and weak
while we got stronger and stronger. We could see the prize from the
platform way up in the stand – could hear it calling to us – all the
time surrounded by red, red and more red.

When the whistle blew, we were jumping and kissing (yep, even
hard old Lloydie) and waving up to the sea of red, as the ever-
faithful Liverpool fans rejoiced in the glory.

And when later, back in Liverpool, we all climbed aboard the big
red bus to parade our trophy in front of our wildly cheering fans
before being welcomed by the Lord Mayor of Liverpool at St
George's Hall, I was blissfully unaware that my days at Liverpool
were numbered, and I only had one person to blame – Larry Lloyd.

CHAPTER 14

LEAVING LIVERPOOL

SO FAR, I had played in every game of the 1973/74 season, so really it should have been no surprise to me that my muscles would begin to complain.

In February 1974, I ruptured my hamstring muscle while playing against Norwich City at Anfield. It heralded a very bad spell for me. It wasn't a small pull. Oh no… but a great big fucking rip! I had ten cortisone injections into my muscles, and the lump is still there today to remind me of this rotten time in my career!

I didn't play again that season. Yes, the season where Liverpool got to the FA Cup final and whooped Newcastle United 3–0 at Wembley. This was the point where it came home to me loud and clear that, if you got an injury or weren't fit, you might as well fuck off and die. Oh, how I wanted to play! But there was no way. At least – I consoled myself – I've played so much this season, and defended us up till the fifth round of the Cup, so I will certainly get to travel down to London with the team and drink in the atmosphere of the FA Cup final with my team-mates. Wrong.

'You can travel down on the coach with the apprentices and players' wives,' Bill Shankly said, without even looking me in the eye.

I knew then that, although he was a great manager in many ways, where this issue was concerned (in my humble opinion anyway), he was totally out of order.

I was later to learn that Brian Clough operated in similar ways – illness and injury were not to be tolerated. I was gutted, and had no fucking intention of travelling to Wembley in the fashion he had suggested. I was NOT a fringe player; I was Liverpool's MAIN centre-half. What was going on?

Don't get me wrong. I had no gripe with Phil Thompson, the player who had taken my place due to the injury. He did a fantastic job switching from midfield. But I blew my top, and told Shanks what he could do with his Saturday-morning coach trip, and I swore to myself in that moment that I would not go to Wembley.

It was an agonising day for me. I tortured myself for hours about what would be going on down in London. The team would be at Hendon Hall the night before, and Bill Shankly would be tucking into the Dover sole fish he loved so much. I was very good at winding myself up. Instead of watching Liverpool walk all over Newcastle, Sue and I went to visit my lovely brother Bill and his wife, Mary, in Colchester – wherever they lived always became my bolthole when I felt under pressure, as they were wonderfully understanding – and we stayed well away from all the victory celebrations when the team returned to Liverpool. Perhaps some might think my attitude was bad, and the media certainly weren't slow to note my absence. They unkindly said I snubbed my team-mates. But that wasn't the case. I was glad for them; I was just pissed off that I had been snubbed. I don't know, the media can get it so wrong at times. Actually, a lot of the time.

The summer came and went, and before I knew it the time had come for pre-season training for the 1974/75 season. I was fully fit and raring to go, but it didn't take me long to sense that all was not well. The message before had always been: 'Larry, you go first to head the ball (defensively) and then you, Emlyn, follow on…' But this time it was: 'Phil, you go first…' I was actually last to be considered. Phil was in the first team and I was in the reserves. I felt sick. This was, in my opinion, a bloody liberty. But I stayed silent and never complained, which was nuts because I never, ever stayed silent. Was I losing my fighting spirit? Then I recognised myself again and fought back. The straw that broke the proverbial camel's back came in the form of a trip to Amsterdam that didn't include yours truly.

I was fuming, really fuming. I charged into Shankly's office, full of rage and indignation. What I didn't realise was that Shanks was preparing to leave Anfield. He was as calm as I was angry and simply told me that he had decided to begin the season with the team who finished the previous season. I stormed out saying I wanted a transfer.

Outside in the corridor I came face to face with Bob Paisley. I thought he was going to try to calm me down, but there was absolutely no chance of that. The now familiar 'red mist' was upon me, and there was no sense of reason when I was in this dangerous frame of mind. But what Paisley said was: 'It's me you need to talk to now, Larry – not Shanks. Bill is winding down, and getting ready to retire.'

I repeated to Paisley that I wanted a transfer.

He firmly answered, 'I can't and won't change an FA Cup-winning side.' He went on to promise me that I would be back in the team by the seventh game – even if they won the first six.

But that wasn't good enough for hot-headed Lloydie! Seeing more of the ominous mist, I yelled, 'Stuff your club!'

He went on, 'You can have a new contract, a higher wage and a four-year extension which means more security for your family.'

'I don't give a fuck about your money,' I hurled back at him. 'I want to be in your fucking team! I want to play football and, if I can't play football, I want a transfer!'

Paisley replied that he didn't want to sell me, that I still had a career at Liverpool. I was still their number-one centre-half. But I was hearing nothing, just seeing the damn red mist that was clouding my judgement. I was hot-headed and full of arrogance, but I just couldn't help myself. I was saying what was real for me, and felt as though I would be betraying my beliefs and stamping on my soul if I backed down. Anyway, I didn't know how to back down. It wasn't in my make-up. I was 25 years of age, and I'd lost my head totally. In my defence, I know I was behaving in this way because of how passionate I was about the game I had always loved.

'Are you sure, Larry?' said Bob

'I'm sure.'

'Then put it in writing.'

I put in a written transfer request, and Liverpool then put a £240,000 transfer fee on my head in the hope of pricing me out of the market; but, wham, in came Coventry with the asking price. Bill Shankly retired in mid-negotiations and, to be honest, the communication was terrible – except for the point I made about him sticking his red shirts up his arse. He understood that bit all right. I understood nothing.

Only much later did I concede that logically it made sense to start the season with a Cup-winning side – but it was too late then. Ah! That wonderful but frustrating thing called hindsight. I wonder how different it might have been if my tantrum hadn't collided with a change of management. Because there was certainly something going on in the background about why Bill Shankly was suddenly retiring. To this day, I don't know why he retired. He got close to telling Emlyn one day, over a drink at his home, but never actually revealed all. I shouldn't have gone – but I did.

It took Coventry's manager, Gordon Milne, a mere two hours to persuade me that joining his club was the right move. He sold me a good story.

So I signed and then immediately regretted my decision. I was being sent to Coventry. That's just what it felt like. You could say I'd cut my nose off to spite my face, because I'm sure I *did* have a future with the Reds – the fantastic club I had been with for five years and had enjoyed so much success. Yet, on the other hand, had I not gone to Coventry, I would probably never have had the opportunity to join Nottingham Forest, under the management of Brian Clough – so some really brilliant times did come my way as a direct result of my hot-headed nature. But that was more luck than judgement.

I was on my way to Coventry – well, at least they were in the First Division – but would they stay there? Were my days in the big time numbered? Or was I going to soar to even greater heights with Coventry? It was a scary, transitional time where I feared my career could take a nose-dive. I'd achieved so much during my five years at Anfield. I had played with the best players and in front of the best fans. Was it game over for Lloydie?

CHAPTER 15

SENT TO COVENTRY

WHAT IN GOD'S name had I done? Highfield Road was not the road for Lloydie. I didn't like anything at all about the set-up there. Don't get me wrong, the manager, Gordon Milne, was a great man, and we remain friends to this day, but everything else was total shit. Nothing felt right. I was out on a limb – a fish out of water, anything but comfortable. Putting it mildly, it crossed my mind, 'What the fuck am I doing here?'

During our transfer talks, Gordon Milne had confided in me that he was also going to put in a bid for Bristol City's Geoff Merrick. Gordon was aware of how much I rated him as a useful player. I remembered him well from my Bristol Rovers days. It made me think that Coventry were an ambitious side and determined to go somewhere, but after I'd signed there was no more mention of the talented Merrick coming to join us.

On the first day of training I felt so lost. I wanted to be back at Liverpool – was *desperate* to be back there with my old team-mates.

It crossed my mind, as I stood in the shower close to tears, and on the verge of a scary panic attack, that if I faked a bad back – an injury I'd had at Liverpool – my transfer would be null and void, and I'd be sent home to everything that was familiar.

Everything that *could* go wrong *did* go wrong, and, when I developed back trouble for real, my time at Coventry was doomed.

I really was flat on my back and with depression setting in fast. I managed to make only 40 club appearances. What an investment I turned out to be – not!

I was always in the press. At first the headlines were complimentary, saying things like 'Left-foot Lloyd Strikes Again' and 'Gunners Beware – Hot Shot Larry is waiting to Gun You Down'. This second was accompanied by a cheesy photograph of me grinning and holding on to a bloody great big cannon. But it wasn't long before I was in the media for all the wrong reasons. Headlines such as 'Angry Larry Misses Cup Tie After Third Booking' and 'Banned Lloyd Must Belt Up' were the order of the day.

Then there was the time I bared my arse to the horrified Ipswich fans, after a sliding tackle that didn't endear the Ipswich crowd to me. That little caper got me into hot water, and I nearly faced a hefty fine and a ban, but due to a photo that was a little bit misleading, and showed only half my backside and the rest covered up, I got away with it.

I have Tommy Hutchinson to thank for the start of my back problem. It happened in training. In spite of it being a freezing cold day, I was not wearing a tracksuit, and Tommy, always the comedian, decided to volley the ball on to the top of my bare legs. My God, did it sting! Determined to get him back, I stooped down to pick up the ball – and was stuck. I couldn't bloody move, and I didn't move much for a very long time.

I had played some of the 1974/75 season, but now, in November 1975, I was out of the game good and proper.

I think the opposite of the wonderment of scoring a goal is being flat on your back with a painful injury, and being scared to death that you'll never walk again. I knew after six weeks on traction with no change that I was in trouble. The pain was excruciating, so, when a top neurosurgeon, Bill Whatmore, walked into my life and diagnosed my problem, I was mightily relieved. I know, without a shadow of a doubt, that it's Bill I have to thank to this day for being able to walk.

He diagnosed a slipped disc. The disc had slipped so far out of the joint that is was pressing on my sciatic nerve. When he suggested he could fix it by operating, I jumped at the chance.

I trusted him implicitly. It's funny how some great surgeons can instil such trust in you, kind of instinctive, and fear melts away when you hear those prized words, 'I can fix you – I know what I'm doing.' This neurosurgeon was going to take great care of my sciatic nerve and I was going to walk again.

Within days, I was transferred to Walsgrave Hospital in Coventry where he successfully performed the operation, and just three days later I was out of bed, albeit with a drip hanging out of my spine. I was still in agony, but thankfully on the mend.

I wasn't the best patient and not the sweetest person to have around. It must have been hell for poor Sue, who had to take care of two young children and then visit a miserable old bastard who had now earned the nickname 'Albert Tatlock', after the grumpy old man in *Coronation Street*.

My angry head just kept on growing. Bill Whatmore might have fixed me physically, but emotionally I was all over the place. I didn't understand at the time, but from my vantage point now I can look back and say I was suffering from deep depression. I had fucked up.

I should never have asked for that damn transfer, and would have turned back the clock if I could. It's a terrible thing when the lightbulb pings on and you realise you've only yourself to blame for being in a bad situation.

When I wasn't picked to be in the first team at Liverpool at the beginning of the season, I was thinking with my left foot. I was kicking arse, shouting my big mouth off and being a pain. What had I been thinking of? Well, that was the problem. I hadn't thought anything through, and I hadn't been listening to advice. Instead, I believed I knew it all. But when I had time to sit and reflect – and time is something you have in abundance when you are flat on your back for weeks on end with only yourself for company – I knew I had fucked up. Being angry with myself wasn't an easy situation to deal with. It takes a hell of a lot of maturity to be able to own up to your mistakes and take responsibility for your actions.

To be able to say, 'Yes, I was wrong, and you were right,' wasn't something I was capable of in my twenties. Now, in my fifties, I can say, 'Fuck me, Lloydie, you messed up good and proper there,' but back then I didn't possess the mind skills.

Regrets and bitterness were killing my soul, and added to this was my terrible fear that I would never play football again. *How was I going to support my family?* This thought was dominant, and I ruminated constantly about our future.

As the days passed with me lying flat on my back, I got worse and worse. Then Bill Whatmore said it was time for me to get up and walk. The pain was still terrific, but at least I had a feeling of movement, of being able to *do* something at last.

The physiotherapy was a painfully slow process for me, but I have a feeling it was worse for the two little nurses who had to help prop up a miserable 14-stone Albert Tatlock, who just kept on growling.

For days, it was a case of right foot, left foot, right foot, left foot, as a professional footballer learned to walk all over again.

The stronger I became physically, the more my head cleared. I had blamed Tommy Hutchinson for the injury, but now I could see it was inevitable I was destined to collapse at some point, and it was nothing to do with his high jinks

I guess at the time I was young and had to blame someone else for my misery. It's so much easier to blame someone else than take responsibility yourself. It's the difference between being a man or a boy. I might have been a man but I often reverted back to being an angry boy when under pressure.

At the age of 26, my back was clearly under strain and the injury was waiting to happen – now I had to fight to get well. My family depended on me, and now I had to use every ounce of determination to get fit again.

The season was coming to an end, and I *would* be ready to play by the time pre-season training began. I *would*. And guess what? I *was* fit in time. It was nothing short of a miracle really – one performed by a genius neurosurgeon.

My playing career was definitely at its lowest ebb when Coventry City tried to sell me to Third Division Walsall. How was this happening? I had trained hard all summer, and by the new season I was as fit as a fiddle, and as ambitious as ever. However, I was not making regular first-team appearances because allegedly big tough centre-halves were no longer in fashion!

Long sideburns were still all the rage, but tough, bold players were, according to Coventry, a thing of the past.

Gordon Milne reckoned solid brick walls like me needed to be replaced by nippy centre-backs, and so he bought two of the buggers in to replace me. Was my career coming to an end? Did I even exist any more? I had been out of the England squad for two years, and now I was out of the headlines altogether.

I don't think anyone either knew or cared whether I was alive or dead. When was I going to escape from the doldrums? But I was stuck in a situation where I had no control over my destiny. I didn't feel there were any choices and no light at the end of the tunnel.

One day I was in the dining room after training when Jimmy Hill sauntered past with this important-looking Arab. He really pissed me off when he turned to the Arab and said in a loud voice, 'This is the player that Liverpool sold us with a bad back.'

I felt humiliated. How dare someone who is supposed to be an icon in the game lower himself and speak in such a demeaning way in public. If he had a problem with me, he should have spoken in confidence and given me a chance to have my say. It just goes to show how badly a bloke can behave when being loyal to his beloved team. And, to be fair, Jimmy Hill was devoted to both Coventry and the game in general.

Four years later, when I was doing well at Nottingham, I bumped into him again when Forest were playing Coventry in a league game. When I say Nottingham were doing well, I mean *really* well. We had won the league as well as the European Cup.

Hill walked over to me in the reception area, leading by his chin as usual, and shook my hand. I wondered whether this was some kind of apology for being so mean before. I think it was.

In Liverpool's defence, my back injury didn't occur until way after the transfer. But anyway – I grinned at Jimmy Hill that day and couldn't help myself gloating a little. 'Oh, Jim!' I crowed. 'I owe you a big vote of thanks. You sold me to Nottingham Forest with a bad back, and now I'd like to show you my medals.'

I know Jimmy Hill is a popular guy and prominent television

personality, but he didn't float my boat. Maybe it was a personal thing; all I know is we clashed. Perhaps the fact that he had criticised me (no, he was downright rude actually!) while I was on a downer made me react so strongly. I know it affected me quite badly.

But, if I'm honest, I did myself no favours while at Coventry. I was unhappy, and messed around a bit. I was always making a nuisance of myself, which, looking back, was nuts, but at the time that was how it was. I'd become a real head banger, and this was probably because I was not at a club where I could grow and thrive, either professionally or personally. I was lost in Coventry, and that was a bad place for me to be.

I felt bad that I couldn't do better for Coventry. After the realisation that I couldn't go back to Anfield, I got on with the job at hand at Coventry.

The last thing I'd needed was that awful back injury. I'm certain I would have got stuck in and played my heart out for the Sky Blues. They were a quality side with great supporters. When I joined them, they were in the First Division – in fact, they were so consistent throughout the last four decades of the 20th century that only Arsenal, Liverpool and Everton can claim to have done better over such a long period. Then Gordon Milne gave me the *really* bad news – Walsall had offered a measly £40,000 for me. 'Wouldn't you like to go?' he asked in all seriousness.

'No, I bloody well wouldn't; I'm looking for something better than that!' Of course I was. Sorry, Walsall, but, as I said, I'm an honest kind of bloke.

Soon I was summoned in again. This time the manager said, 'Cloughie wants you.'

'Who is he managing now?' was my terse response.

'Nottingham Forest.'

Forest were, at that time, sitting mid-table in the Second Division, and that didn't appeal to me a great deal. All I knew about Clough was what I'd seen on TV, and I hadn't been too impressed. I thought he was a mouthy git. But I must admit, the idea of meeting with him ignited some fire inside me.

He wanted me for a month on loan initially, saying it would give me a chance to see if I liked being at Nottingham Forest. He said, 'It's not about us having a look at you, it's about you having a look at us!'

The clever bastard knew I wasn't at all sure about moving to a lower division, so he turned it around to give me a feeling of being in control. He went on to say, 'I'd sign you tomorrow, Larry.' Cunning old Cloughie knew how to play the psychology game.

But I'd also heard he was a good manager and even operated in a similar fashion to Bill Shankly, so I guessed I might feel at home with him. It was worth the powder and shot, anyway.

So I went on loan to Nottingham Forest for the month of October 1976, and I can't tell you how good it felt to be playing regular first-team football. A sense of being wanted once more made me feel like a worthwhile person again. It did me the absolute world of good. I didn't want to leave the First Division, though, but weighed against this was the fact that, if Forest had once been a great team, they could make the grade again, and, if so, I wanted to be there with them to taste the glory.

It was strange because after my month on loan to Forest I went back and experienced the best time I'd ever had with Coventry, and when Clough put in an offer for me I became wobbly. Changes are difficult, and in a way staying felt the safer bet; Sue was relatively happy in Coventry, baby Damian had been born and we were a secure little unit. Did we really want to up sticks and move on to Nottingham?

But Gordon Milne was man enough to be honest with me, and told me that there really was no future for me as I was not nippy enough for the Coventry bunch. Not so for Forest. Milne said to me, 'Forest have been watching you closely since you returned from your month there, and they are desperate to sign you.'

What was the alternative – to stay at Coventry and fester? There was no contest. I had far too much ambition burning inside me. *Big centre-halves out of fashion – my arse!*

A fee of £50,000 was agreed between the clubs, and Cloughie took on the huge gamble of taking on a hot-headed rebel who was in great danger of becoming a has-been, and for that I have to thank him. By the time I left Coventry, my value had dropped dramatically – by almost £200,000.

Could Cloughie possibly revive my flagging career? As I said, he was like Shanks in many ways. I don't think either of them really liked me much as a person, but they certainly respected me for the player I was – one who gave 110 per cent – and to Shanks and Cloughie that was what mattered. I was a man and not a muppet, and, although I was to go on to be one of the most fined players in Forest's history, I was also to play a crucial part in the biggest success in the history of the club. Brian Clough was to take me out of a downward spiral and from a potential has-been to an international star. And I can tell you this, I was by no means the only player deemed to be past his prime that he did this for, as Kenny Burns and Frank Clark could attest to.

To three seasoned players, add terrific midfielders Martin O'Neill and John Robertson, and young players like Tony Woodcock and Garry Birtles, who Cloughie and Peter Taylor plucked from relative obscurity, and the winning formula, not a dead certainty at first, was born.

CHAPTER 16

NOTTINGHAM FOREST AND THE GLORY YEARS

ANYONE WHO WANTED to know about football management at its best should have observed closely the Brian Clough/Peter Taylor duo. They were instinctive and bounced off each other. Peter had the knack of sniffing out the right boys at the right time and brought them home to Cloughie. They were 20 years ahead of their time. Nottingham Forest had always been considered a small club. It began small, and stayed small until Old Big 'Ed and his sidekick Taylor – the duo who had had so much success together at Derby – breezed into City Ground and took command.

To get some idea about just how much Brian Clough and Peter Taylor did for the club, we need to go back to 1865, to the birth of Nottingham Forest.

Local rivals Notts County were formed in 1862, which makes them the oldest professional football team in the whole world; and were, therefore, well established long before the birth of Forest. They boast the invention off the offside rule and are generally considered pioneers of the modern game, and were founder members of the original Football League. Nicknamed The Magpies they wear a black and white kit, and their ground is now at Meadow Lane stadium. Long ago they played in the grounds of the old Nottingham Castle, at Park Hollow, but they needed somewhere bigger. They had an unsettled spell, and moved from ground to ground, including a spell at Trent Bridge Cricket Ground, until they finally found a place that felt like home.

As far as cities go, Nottingham is quite small with only about 300,000 residents, but no bigger sporting city could you find. Every street you walk down you are reminded of not only the two football clubs but also cricket, ice-skating (there is also a national ice-skating rink, and a vast outdoor water-sports park. With the university located just outside the city centre, it is also very much a lively young place.

There is a huge Scottish link to both Nottingham-based football clubs. Notts County's first big star player was a Scotsman, Jimmy Logan, who famously scored a hat-trick in the 1894 FA Cup final when the club defeated Bolton Wanderers 4–1.

Nottingham Forest were founded in 1865 by a group of shinty players (shinty is a team sport played with sticks and a ball from Scottish and Gaelic decent – derived from the Irish game of hurling).

In 1889, while in an association football league called Football Alliance, they won a competition that allowed them to join the Football League.

Forest were a generous club, and helped many of the bigger clubs to achieve their ambition of being successful clubs. They were especially helpful to two teams who were to one day reign supreme in the Premiership – Arsenal and Liverpool. One thing they did was to loan them shirts, and both teams still wear red to this day.

Forest spent the first half of the 20th century in the Second Division, although they did win the FA Cup in 1898 when they triumphed over great rivals Derby County by three goals to one, and then again in 1959 when they beat Luton Town in the same competition. One of their star players was a chap called Roy Dwight, who was the uncle of pop icon Elton John, whose real name is Reg Dwight. By then, Forest had become a bigger team than their now huge rivals – Notts County.

Nottingham Forest hit a depressing low in 1972 when they were relegated from the First Division. Three years later, Cloughie crashed through the City Ground doors and everything changed.

The club's history seems to consist of long spells struggling – often fighting relegation – with intermittent brief spells of glory. In the late thirties, they finished bottom of the league and actually had to seek re-election. But for now the doom and gloom was coming to an end, and a period of excitement and triumph was about to kick in – giving the loyal fans a brilliant few years.

CLOUGHIE AND TAYLOR

It was actually Peter Taylor who had found me. He found most of the players for Forest, and when he studied my play at Coventry he allegedly saw me as 'a destroyer at the back'.

Taylor found the players and Cloughie moulded them. That's how they worked, and it worked well. Peter watched me play, told Cloughie he rated me, and then Cloughie came to get me. They wanted me and I really didn't stand a chance of turning down their offer.

Sometimes Peter would walk up to Cloughie and say, 'I've found another one.'

Cloughie trusted Peter's judgement implicitly, and would get into his car and drive miles to meet the potential prodigy. Rumour has it that he was so determined to sign Archie Gemmill that he literally moved into the soon-to-be Scottish World Cup captain's spare bedroom. He woke early, cooked breakfast, and then refused to go away until Archie signed on the dotted line.

I liked Peter Taylor. I found him to be a naturally funny man. He would always ask any potential team player four questions.

1. Do you drink?
2. Do you smoke?
3. Do you gamble?
4. Do you play around with girls?

He had this belief that if you scored one 'yes' – say you were a drinker – he'd think long and hard but probably sign you. If you scored two, he'd sign with no hesitation. You hit the jackpot if you scored three, because he would be certain to make you captain. Score none you were fucked, but score four and he'd not only sign you but offer you shares in the club!

Why was this? you might think. Well, it was simple, really – he believed all good players had vices, and if you had all four vices he considered you were ALIVE.

I have to say, I'd still go along with this philosophy today. It's all down to personality and getting stuck in.

I got stuck into two of the necessary attributes. I liked a drink and a smoke. I never gambled, and I certainly never played away. Sue thought I did once. Still does. But I never did, Sue – honest.

The thought of going to a team in a lower league was a big turn-off initially. There was also another problem – Clough and I couldn't agree on terms. I must say, he was one of the most difficult men I have ever had the misfortune to negotiate with. This probably had as much to do with our similar stubborn personalities as anything else, although, that said, I think Cloughie's middle name was 'Difficult'.

However, the deal finally struck, I went off to join the Merry Men of Nottingham with a spring in my step.

Sue stayed on in Coventry with Yolanda and Damian. It seemed the best idea for the time being, especially as the kids were at an age when another upheaval wouldn't be good for them.

The Director of Nottingham Forest at that time was a chap called Fred Reacher. What a smashing man! What a lovely family. He, along with his wife, Ida, and children, Sally and Mick, warmly welcomed me into their home and really looked after me. I was seriously grateful for this as I literally knew nobody in the area.

Fred and I, along with some of his other friends, took to playing golf every Wednesday, which was light relief from my heavy football schedule. For some weird reason, Brian Clough used to get annoyed about our close friendship – but, then again, Cloughie could get weird about lots of things. Those of you reading this who knew him well know what I mean, and those of you who didn't will find out as you read on!   The Merry Men of Nottingham were a great bunch of guys. Striker Peter Withe had joined Forest a month before me, so we were the new men. Unfortunately for him, he left us and went to Second Division Newcastle just before our European Cup glory. I bet he's kicking himself that he didn't stay!

Then there was Scottish midfielder John McGovern, whose first love had actually been rugby. Clough first signed him up to play for Hartlepool, before they both moved on to Derby. John moved to Hartlepool when he was just seven years old, and by the time he was 19 he'd become the youngest person to have played in all four divisions of the football league. Hartlepool *and* Derby were promoted – could John now find the same success here at

Nottingham? We all hoped so. John had also won two Scottish Under-23 caps so, as you can see, he was a bloody good player.

When Dave Mackay took over Derby, and let John know he did not figure in his plans, Clough took him on a whirlwind escapade to Leeds United, where they both had disastrous spells. Cloughie didn't endear himself to the club. On his first day of managing them, he told the lads, 'As far as I'm concerned, you can throw all those medals you've won in the bin, because you won them all by cheating.'

It was the same attitude that led him one day to brag, 'When I go, God will have to give up his favourite chair for me,' that alienated Leeds. *Who the fuck does this big-headed bastard think he is?*

Clough famously lasted 44 days at Leeds.

Several decades after the actual events at Elland Road, David Peace wrote his highly acclaimed novel *The Damned United*, which he based closely on facts about Cloughie's time at Leeds. Rumour has it the book is to be made into a movie. If this happens and the film portrays Cloughie how he is described in the book, any viewer would see Cloughie as he really was. This book has been described as a 'football manager's guide to heaven and hell', but it's the analogy of Clough that amuses me and I agree with the most.

'Take the arrogance of Mourinho, add the cussedness of Alex Ferguson, mix, say, with the conviction of Bob Geldof and the chutzpah of Robbie Williams, and you are getting somewhere close,' writes Peace.

It was always going to go wrong for Cloughie at Leeds. Derby County had been Cloughie's first love and the difference between how he managed Derby compared to Don Revie's style at Leeds was huge. Leeds were considered by many to be a dirty, filthy, uninspired team, and it was alleged that no one disliked the team more than Cloughie. The feeling was mutual.

As for John McGovern, he was never going to be accepted by the fanatical Leeds fans as a Billy Bremner replacement.

When Cloughie walked away from Elland Road, he spat, 'This is a terrible day... for Leeds United.' And he honestly meant it. It wasn't a terrible day for Nottingham Forest though!

I have a theory as to why it all went so disastrously wrong for Cloughie at Leeds. I think, had all the above circumstances been fought with Peter Taylor by his side, disaster might have been averted. But Peter had refused to go with him and Clough, always close to the edge, was tipped over it. Only a crazed man would attempt to sell icons such as Norman Hunter and Johnnie Giles, and I believe he simply had a spell of falling apart.

So, Scotsman John McGovern came to Nottingham Forest with Brian Clough, and I'm glad he did. He was an extremely talented player, and just why Leeds let him go baffles me. All I can think is that McGovern got caught up in the hysteria at Leeds. It is also a mystery as to why he never won a Scotland cap – Scotland let one slip by as far as I'm concerned and I'm certain many will agree with me. John was such a hard worker and also a brilliant tackler. He was always ready to support any of us team-mates and I know Cloughie loved this quality about him.

Sammy Chapman was a well-established player at Nottingham Forest when I arrived, and his big claim to fame was that he ended the club's record of 'no player being sent off in 32 years' when he got his marching orders in a game against Leeds in 1971. He played for Forest for 14 years, and made 350 appearances before he was transferred to rivals Notts County.

Geordie man Frank Clark came to us after a long and illustrious career at Newcastle where they won the old Inter-City Fairs Cup in 1969. What a great full-back! He had come to the attention of

Peter Taylor following a tip-off from a north-east journalist. As with me, critics were saying he was past his best; we were both praying they were wrong. All in all, Frank played 155 matches for Forest and later he was to take over as Cloughie's successor and manage at the City Ground. Much to the delight of club, players and fans, he won promotion for the club and then took them into the top three of the Premiership to win a place in Europe. Not bad for a supposed has-been!

Local lad little Sutton Ian 'Bomber' Bowyer came home after a spell away. He had originally signed with Nottingham Forest in 1968 where he trained as an apprentice, before going off to play with both Manchester City and Leyton Orient as a striker. But during my time and thereafter he was ultimately a powerhouse in midfield, but also a player who intuitively saw an opportunity to strike the ball and score. These qualities really summed him up as the phenomenal player he was – and he remains a great guy who is much loved by all at Nottingham Forest.

Tony Woodcock was another local boy. Tony was initially loaned out to Lincoln City and Doncaster Rovers before finally achieving his dream and breaking into his home club's first team. Under the management of old boss Allan Brown, first-team play seemed to be just a fingertip away and it took the sharpness of his play and the astute eye of Cloughie to ensure his ambitions were realised. It wasn't until Cloughie arrived at Nottingham Forest that Tony became a regular first-team player – the wise old bird realised straight away what a talent he was. He was on fire, always darting here there and everywhere. What an essential he was in our team.

It was a great privilege for me to play alongside such talent. He and I were really at opposite ends of the spectrum – yes, he moved with lightning speed and was one of the most intelligent players to grace

132

the pitches of not only the north and south of England (he played for Arsenal where he made 131 league appearances, scoring 56 goals, and won 42 England caps, scoring 16 goals) but also Europe. It was in October 1979 that Tony broke the German transfer record, when FC Cologne paid £500,000 for his services. Not bad, eh?

What can I say about former Scottish footballer John Robertson, the man who was to become my very best friend? He was a great attacker of the ball in midfield for Forest. John, better known to his mates as Robbo, had played for Scotland as a schoolboy, and then in the youth side, before moving on to being a much valued member of the full Scottish national team.

He made his debut for Forest in October 1970, but was having limited success in midfield and had actually been on the transfer list when Cloughie took over, but that all stopped when Cloughie moved Robbo out on to the left wing to utilise his amazing football skills. Our new and enthusiastic manager quite rightly said, 'John became one of the finest deliverers of the ball I have ever seen – in Britain or anywhere else in the world – as fine as the Brazilians or the supremely gifted Italians.'

Robbo still lives in Nottingham today and is Martin O'Neill's number two at Aston Villa. They have an amazing friendship and understanding of each other and I know for sure that one of John's happiest times (outside Nottingham of course) was with Martin O'Neill and Celtic. He has a great love for Celtic, a great love for Nottingham and a great love for his family and children. He also has a great love for me, but we've never hugged off the pitch, only on it when one of us scores – him more than me of course!

Robbo was singled out by Clough – after transforming him from midfielder to world-class winger – as the man who made Forest tick. During the seventies and eighties (1970–82), John Robertson played 374 games for Nottingham Forest and several years later he popped back to the City Ground, much to the joy of the fans, to play in 11 more matches.

I guess, out of all us merry men, it's Kilrea-born Martin O'Neill who is best known today – as he continues to have a fantastic career. He joined Nottingham Forest in 1971 from Derry City and was brilliant in midfield.

From 1971 to 1984, he played 64 internationals for Northern Ireland, scoring eight goals. Although he preferred a role in midfield he was often to be found out on the right wing where he would surge forward and score many goals.

Martin is an interesting guy off the pitch too, very well educated. Gaelic football was his first passion, and he played to a high level. But later on was accused of breaching the Gaelic Athletic Association by playing 'foreign sports'.

Cloughie described Martin as being 'bright, sharp, and a right smart arse. Someone fully prepared to stand his ground and answer back when he believed he was right.' Needless to say, Martin and Cloughie clashed a lot.

On one occasion, Cloughie infuriated Martin by substituting him after he'd scored two goals and he was chasing a hat-trick. Clough turned to Jimmy Gordon (his trainer at the time), and told him, 'He's coming off, or we play with two balls – one so he can carry on showing off, and the other for the rest of the team.'

But Cloughie recognised just how much enthusiasm Martin had for football, and what he had given up in pursuit of his first love.

Viv Anderson was yet another Nottingham boy born and bred. The story of his youth is more than worthy of a mention here, especially for any young readers who are desperate for a career in the sport they feel passionately about.

Viv was an avid Manchester United fan as a child and his dream was initially to play for them (I think we can forgive him). Can you imagine his delight when, at the age of 15, Manchester United recognised his talent and approached him for a trial, but he chose to finish his education first and by the time he went back and knocked on the door it was a 'thanks but no thanks'. Rejected and totally devastated, he threw it all in and got a 'proper' job at the local printers.

Obviously, he didn't stop playing football and, sure enough, along came a Nottingham Forest scout and that, as they say, was that. He got lucky and Nottingham Forest got lucky. He signed as an apprentice in 1974 and, although he was a full-back, he was handy in almost every position. He was stunning in attack, sound in defence and wonderful in the air.

What a privilege it was for me to get to know him as a man and play football with a footballer so talented that he also got to play for Manchester United, Arsenal, Sheffield Wednesday, Barnsley and Middlesbrough – and, of course, England, for whom he played for a decade and won 30 caps. Not bad – thank God, he didn't stay at the printers!

He was also the first black guy to play for England. The racist shit must have been difficult for Viv sometimes, but he was made of strong stuff. He knew who he was and what he was worth – the sum being priceless. It will come as no surprise then to learn he has played a huge role in the progress of black footballers who have followed in his footsteps into top-flight football.

What a full-back – and what a star – he was, especially in the two European Cups we won. Not only was he a brilliant defender of the game but he could also attack and was great in the air. As you can imagine, he is still adored at Nottingham Forest. In 1997, 96 per cent of the fans voted him into Forest's All-Time Greats XI. Viv Anderson was awarded the MBE in 1999 for services to football.

Garry Birtles was another local boy. Can you believe Cloughie paid a mere £2,000 for him when he plucked him from non-league side Long Eaton? Here we had another case of Peter Taylor being sharp and brilliant at discovering raw talent. Garry had been a carpet fitter and he soon became a Clough favourite and I have to say Cloughie got the best out of Garry in the same way as he got the best out of me.

Clough zoomed in to snap up Trevor Francis from Birmingham City for a staggering £1,000,000. (I guess he could afford it after the bargain deal he'd had with Garry Birtles!) When he was asked by the media if any footballer could possibly be worth that amount, he naturally said, 'Of course.' Old Big 'Ed could say nothing else.

Trevor was an agile and skilful forward, who had spent some time in America playing for the Detroit Express. He had negotiated a secondment from Birmingham to allow him this experience – but now he was *really* going to have an experience. We all were.

Then there was dear old Archie Gemmill – a more competitive player I'll never know. Another Scotsman, he began his career with St Mirren, but it was while playing for Preston that he came to the attention of Cloughie, who was so determined to sign him for Derby that he actually slept at Archie's house to make sure he didn't go and sign elsewhere! And Archie didn't go elsewhere. Instead, he went everywhere Cloughie went – to Derby, to Nottingham Forest and if Cloughie had gone to Timbuktu he'd have probably gone there with him as well – along with John McGovern and John O'Hare (another terrific player who remained loyal, shadowing Cloughie from Derby to Leeds and then Forest).

Gary Mills was the youngest player – he was 18 years of age – to ever play in a European Cup final when Trevor Francis was injured,

136

giving him the opportunity to shine in midfield. What a result for the boy.

Peter Shilton — well, what can I say that hasn't already been said? The man is a bloody hero, legend, icon and a fabulous man. He signed for Forest from Stoke in 1977 and what a prize they purchased. He was Forest goalie until 1982 — special and important years, years of the like they may never see again — although I sincerely hope they do. He made 202 appearances and I was out there on that pitch with him for four seasons of them (1977–81). In Nottingham Forest's Championship year in 1977, he let in only 18 goals in 37 appearances.

I agree with the majority when I say he is the best goalkeeper England has ever seen, but I also believe his best days were while he was with Forest and playing under the Clough/Taylor management. He was later to be awarded the MBE and then the even higher accolade of CBE. Not a bad career. Not a bad goalie to be standing behind you in case you fuck up!

And then there was the handsome and delicate Kenny Burns. Not! Kenny was about as handsome and delicate as yours truly, but at least I had teeth! Kenny was renowned for his 'wild boy' image and he played up to it. He and I were, honest to God, the most formidable pair to play in the central-defence areas. We terrified the opposition and often won the ball by intimidation and brute force.

MY DEBUT GAME

My debut game for Forest came during my initial loan period. It was against Hull City, and we lost 1–0. Fucking hell, did I ever get a shock!

I had always been popular with the general public. Even when I ousted hero Ron Yeats at Liverpool, I was respected for the tough player I was. Fans had always known that I was one of them – a loyal kind of 'what you see is what you get' type.

But I'd been a latecomer to the Hull City game, and Sammy Chapman, the absolute legend I just told you about, who had been there *forever*, had been listed in the programme as playing. When the team was read out over the tannoy, and it was announced that Larry Lloyd was to wear the coveted No.5 shirt, all hell broke loose.

'Who the fuck is Larry Lloyd?' was the question burning the lips of the supporters. The booing was the loudest I ever remember hearing – probably because it was aimed at me. It was bloody horrible. I still remember my thoughts. *Hey, what do you mean, 'Who the fuck is Larry Lloyd?' What's going on? I'm ex-Liverpool for Christ's sake*. Oh, I felt very ordinary and my bruised ego was hurting badly, as for 90 minutes my new team's fans sang out, 'Oh… Sammy Chapman.' How I managed to play beats me, and the fact that I had a decent game is nothing short of a miracle. I was devastated.

Billy Bremner was on loan to Hull, and he scored the winning goal which went down like a lead balloon with Cloughie. He and Clough clashed badly. There was no love lost between these two opinionated guys. Cloughie told me he would never sign Bremner – not even if he was gift-wrapped.

WINNING PROMOTION TO THE FIRST DIVISION 1976/77 AND IN THE FIRST DIVISION 1977/78

Forest were tenth in the Second Division when I signed, but Cloughie's plan was coming together nicely as we speedily climbed the table. He said Nottingham Forest had been like a stagnant pool when he blasted into the club and said he was going to eliminate the pollution and make it fresh again.

He had plucked his new side from here, there and everywhere — men who were hungry for success and silverware, and who shared his passion and determination, and as he said, 'men who could actually play football'.

We worked hard for each other, and the work paid off, for by the end of the season promotion all hinged on the last match. We couldn't affect the outcome. With all our games played, we were level on points with Bolton, who were due to play at home to Wolverhampton Wanderers. Wolves had already won the title, and we thought we had little chance of going up. Our team was actually away on holiday in Majorca and I was due to join them the following day.

There was a feeling among us all that Wolves wouldn't try too hard. They didn't need to bother, as the title win and promotion was all wrapped up for them.

My family and I were still living in Coventry, so that day I went to watch a match at Highfield Road. Later, I was in the players' lounge with my son Damian, when the news filtered through that Wolves had unexpectedly beaten Bolton, which meant we were promoted. I couldn't believe it! Bolton had only needed a point. It was champagne and celebrations all over again for Sue and me. We were ecstatic.

That summer, Clough bought three great players. Our new goalie was, in my opinion, *the* best goalie *ever* — the one and only Peter Shilton.

Our team was now complete and ready to rock and roll. Not everyone agreed though. According to the media, we were going to be the 'also-rans' of the First Division — a team made up of rebels, has-beens and no-hopers.

So there I was, at the ripe old age of 26, being written off yet again by the press. They made the wrong assumption my successful days were over. Hadn't they heard the story about the fat lady singing? Well, she *was* still in fine voice, and *I* was in great shape and fantastic spirits.

We boys at the City Ground were up for the challenge, and challenge we did. Oh! How we proved those critics wrong. Being an unknown quantity we managed to take the other clubs by surprise – and we took the First Division by storm. In every single game, we just went all out for victory, and the wins just kept on coming.

My fortune had turned full circle. From being an out-of-favour player at Coventry, I became one of the heroes of another European Cup-winning side. Yes – that's right, *European*!!

That first year in the top flight, we spectacularly won the league Championship and the League Cup – beating Liverpool, of all teams, in a thrilling 1–0 win in an Old Trafford replay after drawing 0–0 at Wembley. Thus began four tremendous years at Nottingham Forest.

The following season we retained the League Cup, defeating Southampton 3–2 at Wembley.

Then in the 1978/79 season we went steaming into Europe. Poor old Martin O'Neill and Archie Gemmill were recovering from injuries and trying to convince Cloughie that they were fit. Poor bastards, it's terrible when you're injured at the time of a big tournament. I knew that one well from my Liverpool days and missing that FA Cup match against Newcastle. When Cloughie said an emphatic 'NO', Martin said, 'But I'm as right as rain', and Archie yelled, 'Fuck you.'

Nottingham Forest, with or without two of their stars, were off to Europe.

THE EUROPEAN CUP 1978/79

The first opponents we found ourselves up against in the draw for the European Cup were my old team and reigning European Champions, Liverpool.

Although we had finished seven points clear of them in the league, they were the club everyone expected to do well. Their reputation went before them – especially in cup ties. The first leg was played at City Ground and if we had two things going for us it was that we were at home with the brilliant Forest fans in full song and we possessed the element of surprise. Nobody knew who new boy Garry Birtles was, and it was Garry who would shock them into reality. Nottingham Forest were a team to be reckoned with.

Garry gave us the lead after 27 minutes of us dominating them. Liverpool made a defensive error and the new kid on the block rushed on in and scored.

Colin Barratt, who had joined Forest from Manchester City in 1976 and could literally play in any position, volleyed the ball home for a 2–0 lead to take to Anfield for the second leg.

The press still had Liverpool as favourites but we weren't listening. We were on a mission. We were going to go to Anfield and whoop arse. Well, there may have been no goals but that was fine with us! We were pretty damn good in defence and wouldn't let Liverpool play their usual game of flair: 0–0 – we were through to the next round.

There were lots of upsets in this first round. Bruges, the Belgian finalists and runners-up to Liverpool the year before, were knocked out by Polish team Wilsa and Juventus were knocked out by Glasgow Rangers.

When it came to the second round, there were no changes. More shocks, devastation and whoops of delight sounded around Europe when Real Madrid went crashing out to Grasshoppers of Zurich. Also out were the Dutch side PSV Eindhoven (they too were victims of Glasgow Rangers) and Dynamo Kiev.

We were up against AEK Athens, and in the away leg we won 2–1, with John McGovern and Garry Birtles scoring the goals. It wasn't an easy game to play in. The crowd of 36,000 were really hostile, setting off flares and generally letting us know in no uncertain terms that we weren't welcome. But in the home leg we really let them have it by winning 5–1. Garry Birtles scored two this time while David Needham got one, as did Tony Woodcock and Viv Anderson.

In March, we played Grasshoppers of Zurich in the quarter-final. The home match was brilliant. We whooped them 4–1 and I scored! Fabulous. Garry Birtles was back on the score sheet again as was my mate Robbo (from a penalty) and Archie Gemmill. In the away match, Martin O'Neill put one in the back of the net and the score was a draw at 1–1. We were through to the semi-finals. It felt terrific – especially as we were firm underdogs.

SEMI-FINALS

By the semi-final stage, the four teams left with dreams of winning the title were Austria Vienna, Malmo, Cologne and us, Nottingham Forest.

As we went into our semi-final against Cologne, we were in a very upbeat mood. The only blot on the horizon was that we were missing Kenny Burns and Viv Anderson, but when we kicked off for the first leg at City Ground we were surprised how attacking they were. It was unusual for an away team to come at you. They must have been taking advantage of our losses in defence. It wasn't long before we were two goals down. Could this spell disaster? Hey, we're talking about Nottingham Forest here – us Glory Boys of the seventies knew how to get stuck in. Before Cologne knew what was happening, Ian Bowyer had a shot on a target and the baby flew into the back of the net; and then Robbo and Garry Birtles got a header a piece. Bang! 3–2.

We were hanging on in there with one of those small leads that keep your heart pumping with fear in case the other side comes back at you. It only takes one breakaway – one frantic moment and it can all change. We saw that in the 1966 World Cup final. We've seen it a million times at all levels of football from grass roots to the top.

Then Cologne sent on a substitute – a Japanese boy named Yasuhiko Okudera (how's that for a memory of an old-timer!) who scored a late equaliser with a 25-yard shot that came from nowhere and seemed to just slide under Peter Shilton's body. It was quite bizarre.

So the first leg ended in a 3–3 draw. It was an exciting game for the neutral but scary for us and our fans. They had scored three away goals and must have been delighted.

At the press conference after the game, I remember Cloughie being brilliant as he stared directly into the TV camera and, full of his usual arrogance, stated, 'If anyone out there thinks that Nottingham Forest are out, they had better think again.'

Now we had to go and play the second leg… away. We travelled to Germany, dug in and got down and dirty. People were beginning to fear us in our away matches. We were inspired and somehow Cloughie keyed us up for these matches.

During this match, we were brilliant in defence; in fact, I'd go as far as to say that this was the best defensive display in the whole of this particular European Cup. And I'm not joking. Anyone around today who was there back in 1979 will tell you the same – and if they want to challenge me I'm up for it.

We had Viv and Burnsie back to help us keep a clean sheet but we needed a breakthrough – we *had* to score. We won a corner, I flicked the ball over to Ian Bowyer and he headed home. Yep – I'd only set up the winner! And, more importantly, we were only in the bloody European Cup final!

THE 1979 EUROPEAN CUP FINAL

Nottingham Forest v Malmo, Olympic Stadium, Munich, 30 May 1979
Attendance: 57,000
Team – Peter Shilton, Viv Anderson, Frank Clarke, John McGovern (captain), Larry Lloyd, Kenny Burns, Trevor Francis, Ian Bowyer, Garry Birtles, Tony Woodcock, John Robertson.
Manager: Brian Clough.

Some idiots said we were a small club and were lucky to have made it to the final. Then there were critics who reckoned we were playing another 'small' club that were also not at full strength, as their best defenders Bo Larsson and Roy Andersson were injured and their captain, midfielder Staffan Tapper, had broken his toe in training on the day before the match.

While it was true that neither of us were giants in Europe, what *was* true was that we'd beaten giants to get to the final. In one of the earlier rounds, we had lost to Dynamo Berlin at the City Ground 1–0 and then when we travelled to Germany for the second crucial leg we won 3–1. It hadn't been an easy away game either on or off the pitch. We had known it wasn't going to be good enough for us to play a defensive game. We had to score goals – and score goals we did. Trevor scored two and then Robbo slotted one home – happy days.

It was freezing though – I mean, fucking freezing. I was the coldest I had ever been in my entire life. Had we been able to wear gloves and tights (now there's a vision of loveliness – and I don't mean me, I mean Burnsie), we might have defrosted a little, but can you imagine Cloughie allowing us to wear thermals? I don't think

144

so. If he'd caught us wearing what he considered to be 'nancy clothes', he would have fined us on the spot.

But on 30 May 1979 there was nothing soft about us. We might have been the Merry Men of Nottingham, but woe betide anyone that stood in our way. We were bringing that Cup home if it was the last thing we did.

There were 57,000 spectators in the crowd in the Munich Olympic Stadium, which means it was nowhere near full. Those present were about to watch two teams from whom they really didn't know what to expect. The Nottingham Forest fans that had travelled across Europe to support us were, as usual, very vocal singing our club song of 'Robin Hood, Robin Hood, riding through the glen... Robin Hood, Robin Hood with his band of men...'

It was clear from the first blow of the whistle that the Swedish side Malmo were going to play a defensive game. Well, that was OK with us because we had something – or should I say *someone* – up our sleeve: Trevor John Francis.

Three months prior to reaching this final, Cloughie had spent the money the club earned from winning the league, and winning a place in the European Cup for the first time, on Birmingham's Trevor Francis. In this ground-breaking transfer, Cloughie made Trevor the first ever million-pound footballer. It was looked upon by many as an extraordinary deal.

Under the UEFA rules, however, it is stipulated that the player involved in the transfer cannot play for their new team in Europe for the first three months. The three months were up just in time for the final for Trevor to make his European debut for Forest. With poor old Martin O'Neill and Archie Gemmill out through injuries, Cloughie selected Trevor to play out on the right wing. It was an inspired decision.

The game wasn't exactly electric. It was all about whether we could break through their wall of defence. At first it seemed impossible, until, with half-time approaching, Robbo found a little space on the left wing and crossed a superb ball over to a waiting Trevor Francis who pounced on it and nodded it in at the far post – GOAL! The Malmo goalkeeper didn't stand a chance! What a time to score!

Those Nottingham Forest fans who had thought the fee for Trevor had been too much now thought again. As Cloughie had told his critics when asked if any player could possibly be worth this much money, 'Yes, if the player helps you achieve success – anyway, if we decide to sell him, we'll get more back than we paid out. It's an investment.' It certainly was.

The second half was all about defence again. It is true it wasn't an exciting final for the fans – indeed, for the nation. But all we cared about was getting the job done and winning, and we had won Europe's biggest prize.

We had shown the whole world what great man-management and closely knit teamwork could achieve. We had also ensured we'd be back again the next year to defend our title.

After the match we were all in the dressing room. Elated is not a strong enough word to sum up our jubilant feelings. Euphoric – that's better. Then Cloughie came in and put the biggest dampener on it by saying, 'Right, lads, put all your medals on the table. I'm having them all.'

We were waiting for him to laugh, and say, 'Only kidding.' But then he told us we'd only been allocated 16 medals and there weren't enough to go round – for the trainers etc.

I dived into the shower, taking my medal with me. He was not going to get his hands on *my* medal. Archie Gemmill and Frank

Clark took theirs too – but some handed them over. Mugs. So there were half a dozen sitting in the middle of the table waiting for him to get his grubby hands on. What a liberty!

1979 EUROPEAN SUPER CUP (UEFA SUPER CUP)

In 1979, we won the European (UEFA) Super Cup, which is an annual game between the winners of the Cup Winners Cup and the European Cup. Nowadays, the final is played in one single match, but back in 1979 and 1980 (in fact, right up until 1998) it was played over two legs. Because it takes place in August, at the beginning of the domestic season, some clubs don't always field their strongest sides – but not us. Silverware is silverware and to win a *Super* medal to add to my collection was not to be scoffed at.

We were up against Barcelona as they had won the Cup Winners Cup. We ended up winning 2–1 on aggregate and collected yet another medal to add to our growing trophy cabinets in our front rooms – far away from Cloughie's grasp.

EUROPEAN CUP 1979/80

As you can imagine, everyone at Nottingham Forest was full of anticipation and excitement as the build-up to the European Cup began to gather momentum. For us to pull it off a second time was probably more than our brilliant fans could wish for. But wishing we all were, and praying to God to throw us some luck to run alongside our hard work ethic. Could we retain the trophy? It was a tall order. But we weren't a wild card this year – we were reigning champions and if anyone thought our win the previous year had been a fluke they'd better watch out. It was game on.

There was no dangerous Liverpool to have to face in the first round. Instead, we were up against another Swedish team called

Oesters Vaxjo (that wonderful memory of mine again). Oesters Vaxjo had beaten Malmo in the race for the Swedish league title, so they were no pushover. Any teams that get into Europe – famous big clubs and small fry alike – are dangerous, we had proved that. And when we beat this Swedish team 3–1 in the first round we confirmed that we were still firing on all cylinders. They had not been easy games; in fact, the scoreline didn't reflect just how tight the games were. We progressed thanks to one particular inspiring save by Peter Shilton and two goals by Ian 'Bomber' Bowyer. In the away fixture, substitute Gary Mills set up a goal for Tony Woodcock and a huge feeling of relief was shared by players and fans alike.

The second round saw us up against an unknown Romanian side called Arges Pitesti (I can pronounce these as well, you know!). They had the reputation of being crap away from home and so it was no surprise when we raced into the lead at City Ground and whooped them 2–0, with Tony Woodcock and Garry Birtles being the guys to get on the score sheet.

At one crucial point in the second-leg away match, I managed to get my head on to a corner ball from Robbo and nod it over to Bomber who scored a cracker. It was Bomber's third goal of this tournament. Then we made it 2–0 when a typical Tony Woodcock cross came flying over to Garry Birtles who dutifully scored.

A dodgy incident involving my mate Burnsie almost spoiled the day when he fouled one of their strikers (memory gone – can't for the life of me remember his name) and they were awarded a penalty. But, fortunately, we had done enough; we were through.

The quarter-finals were no pushover, and we were up against the rough and tough Dynamo Berlin. Well, that was all right – they were up against equally rough and tough Nottingham Forest. That said, we had a bloody hard time against them and when Hans Jurgen

Riediger scored to put them in the lead you could have heard a pin drop at the City Ground.

There wasn't much to sing about when we travelled to freezing-cold Berlin for the second leg either. We had just lost 1–0 to Wolves in the League Cup and were still a bit flat – especially Trevor Francis as he'd come in for a lot of flack. But it wasn't to last and Trevor was about to silence his critics by playing out of his skin.

He was inspired and after just 16 minutes he'd scored a terrific goal. Then just before half-time he made it two. We were in the lead now and our spirits were flying high once more. I tell you, we never stayed down in the doldrums for long – and that was perhaps one of the elements that made us so tough to beat. Then we were awarded a penalty and good old Robbo put it away. Blinding night! Freezing fucking cold still without thermals and tights but who cared – we were hard bastards all over again. We wanted to get our hands on that trophy and make history and we were going to give it our all.

Dynamo Berlin pulled a goal back but I can honestly say there was no way we were going to allow them back into this game – not with the semis in touching distance for a second year on the trot.

SEMI-FINAL

Now we met the mighty Ajax – first at home and then away. The first goal went in ten minutes before half-time and was a classic Robertson/Francis affair, with Robbo swinging the ball across from a corner and Trevor putting the ball in the back of the net. Their keeper, Pete Schrijvers (crikey, these names are tricky), didn't stand a chance. Then Trevor wove a little more of his magic to win a penalty; Robbo had no trouble scoring from the spot.

So off to the Olympic Stadium we went for a return leg in front of a 60,000 crowd. Once again, a stalwart defensive performance from us managed to hold Ajax to a goalless match until halfway through the second half when their striker Lerby's head found the ball which in turn found the back of the bastard net. *Now* the pressure was really on. Cloughie had been right – he had always maintained we should have scored three goals at home to give us the added cushion. But we dug in, with Ajax coming on to us relentlessly, wave after wave, the pressure building... until, finally, sweet relief – that final beautiful whistle blew. We were in the final again!

Nottingham Forest were firing on all cylinders all over again and the 'little' team from England were standing as tall as giants – well, some of us anyway.

THE 1980 EUROPEAN CUP FINAL

Nottingham Forest v Hamburg SV, Santiago Bernabeu, Madrid, 28 May 1980 Attendance: 50,000

Two weeks prior to our date with Hamburg I played in my fourth – and final – match for England against Wales. As you'll see in the next chapter, it wasn't one of my better nights and, to cap it all off, with about twenty minutes to go Welsh hero Terry Yorath clobbered me in a late tackle. The painful result was me nursing damaged ankle ligaments and missing a pre-match trip to Majorca with Cloughie and the lads – just my luck! Instead I stayed in England and had injections and extensive treatment in an effort to get fit.

When they returned I started training once more with the team and declared myself fit for the final. Cloughie did not believe I had recovered so quickly, and he was quite right. The ankle was still swelling up, but there was no way I was going to miss playing in such an important match.

The suspicious Cloughie decided to give me a fitness test with a difference. Every time he walked past me, he rapped me on the ankle to see if I responded with an agonising groan. It hurt – of course it did – but I didn't react. At least not until he was out of sight that was – some bloody fitness test!

On the night of the final, it was stiflingly hot, and we were due to clash with Kevin Keegan's Hamburg SV, the German league leaders. Kevin Keegan was playing up front, and in all honesty Clough was expecting us to get hammered.

I fancied a wind-up in the tunnel, and an idea came to me in a flash, involving lunatic Kenny Burns and my old team-mate Keegan.

As we were lining up, I found myself next to Kevin Keegan, whom, of course, I knew very well. We shook hands and exchanged pleasantries, and then a thought hit me. 'Look, Kev, we know each other well, and I'll be honest with you – we've got a game plan. All I'm going to tell you is this – Kenny Burns will be marking you and we've both agreed that he's gonna kick the shit out of you.'

With that, his jaw dropped; but I wasn't finished. 'Just look at him if you don't believe me,' I said and pointed to Kenny at the back of the line.

As luck would have it, my timing was perfect, because Kenny, who fell out of the ugly tree and hit every branch on the way down, was just removing his teeth and ramming some pink chewing gum in, which looked – for the life of me – like raw meat.

Kevin's face was classic – *OH SHIT!*

The match was extra special as it was the 25th anniversary of the European Cup final, but sadly Trevor Francis, who had scored the previous year, was laid up with a torn achilles tendon, while Hamburg's formidable Horst Hrubesch was nursing an ankle injury, so the pair of them had to sit on the bench watching, not a happy place to be.

Kick off! Hamburg piled on the pressure right from the word go, but, for any of you who remember this match, you may recall that, although Kevin began the game in his usual position up front, after four horrendous tackles from Kenny and a couple from yours truly, it wasn't long before he had shifted to centre-half. It seemed to me that Kevin had taken heed of the words of warning spoken by us nasty bastards in the tunnel.

Hamburg, for all their tremendous efforts, couldn't put a goal away.

We, on the other hand, rarely left our half. But then it happened. In the 21st minute and during our first venture up front, Garry Birtles, who was out on the left, passed to Robbo just as he arrived at the penalty area. Robbo, cool as you like, simply struck with his right foot. Goal!

We played a blinder for the rest of the match and they just couldn't get past our defence. Garry Birtles was charged up and firing on all cylinders, running around up front on his own like a whirling dervish. (Dating back to Turkey in the 13th century, a dervish is a character who allegedly travels, whirling in ecstasy through a mystical journey ascending through mind and love to reach perfection. They spin until they are exhausted – that's good old Garry Birtles for you!)

As for us four at the back, never before had we been such a solid brick wall; we were awesome, even if I do say so myself. We gave the performance of a lifetime and none of the attackers could get past me or Kenny – least of all Kevin Keegan. Reports recalled that 'Kenny Burns and Larry Lloyd stopped nearly every attack that the opposition could throw at them.' You bet we did! It was one of those magical moments when everything comes together perfectly.

Shilton was magnificent in saving the one real chance that Keegan managed to carve out for himself and there's no denying that Hamburg were a skilful side with flair – but we did what we did best and our true grit, determination and hard work ethic won the day. Scaring the life out of their star player in the tunnel helped of course!

When we lifted that trophy high in the sky it was déjà vu all round – we had achieved what had appeared to be the impossible dream. You see, anything is possible.

We were on a high and looking forward to celebrating out on the town with our wives. Clough and Peter Taylor had other ideas though. They had booked us men into a chalet-type place 40 miles north of Madrid, while our WAGs (the wives and girlfriends in those days all wore fur coats, so we nicknamed them 'the furry girls and no knickers brigade' – all in good humour of course) were staying in a fantastic five-star hotel in the city centre. Well, let me tell you something: when you reach the final of a huge cup tie you expect – win, lose, or draw – to party on down afterwards. There is so much energy pumping around your body that it is impossible to come back down until you've let off some steam.

After showering, Clough barked, 'OK, boys, you've got a bit of press to do – then I'll see you on the bus in, say, twenty.'

'What about our wives?' someone was brave enough to ask, to which the stern reply was: 'All on the bus or you're all fired. I want the team to stay together tonight.'

We were furious, and I think we cursed all the way back to the chalet. One or two of the blokes managed to get messages through to their wives, but don't forget this was pre-mobile-phone days. By the time we reached this family-run, very lovely, but not exactly what we wanted, chalet, we were drowning in our misery.

Give this Spanish family their due, they had put on a smashing spread, lobster – the lot. But none of us felt like eating. It was such a total waste. 'Oh, fuck it,' we all cursed for the umpteenth time.

Can you imagine this happening today? You can just see John

Terry and Frank Lampard waving goodbye to their other halves in the centre of Madrid and going back to their digs for a bit of grub before retiring without so much as a glass of champagne.

But retire Clough and Taylor did. 'I'm off to bed,' said Brian, and Taylor followed behind.

The rest of us all looked at each other. No bright lights, no booze, no women and no sex. Then we leaped into action. We searched out the son of our Spanish hosts and asked him if he could drive. He did. Did he have a car? He did. Yessssssss. He was the proud owner of a little Seat. Hmmmm.

So, with the promise to the boy of a fistful of pesetas, we all piled in. The driver and five of us piled into the little Seat. Robbo sat on my lap in the front, while Martin O'Neill, Frank Gray and David Needham all crammed into the back.

Oh, it was a horrendous drive. We set off at midnight and finally chugged into the bright lights of the Spanish capital at one in the morning.

We made our way to the hotel where the wives were hanging out. Robbo rang ahead of our arrival, and whooped, 'We're on our way, girls!'

With all the wives congregated in one room, the fun and laughter began – and it didn't stop. We were too knackered for sex, but were well up for a booze. The mini-bar went in one swoop, and then we rang down for six bottles of champagne – then six more – and so it went on until dawn broke.

There was another dawning as well. It dawned on us on our way back in the taxi (the Spanish boy and the Seat were long gone – thank God!) that we had all been partying in *one* room, and no one had paid the bill. The Nottingham Forest commercial manager, John Carter, would, we knew, go ballistic.

The four of us got back at about 7.30am (David Needham had gone back earlier – I can't remember why, I was too pissed). We staggered into the reception where the cleaner was vacuuming, which hurt our heads. We were rat-arsed. We just about managed to climb on to four high stools at the bar, and then ordered four cups of coffee, the aroma of which was heavenly.

At eight o'clock, Peter Taylor strolled in, took one look at us perched on our stools and muttered, 'How you lads could sit up all night at that bar defeats me.'

Yes. There *was* a God.

However, we were rumbled later, as a very disgruntled John Carter angrily accosted us at the airport.

We didn't lose any sleep over it (but sleep we did on that plane), knowing that not only the club would pay the bill, but that they bloody well *should*. We'd won the bastard European Cup... again! Boring, boring Clough, huh!

1980 EUROPEAN SUPER CUP

Once again we were treating what was considered to be a minor Cup final very seriously. It was an honour to be playing up there with the great teams such as Valencia, whom we now found ourselves against.

In an exciting first leg at City Ground, we thrilled the fans by beating the Spanish side 2–1. But over there the story was different and we lost by a whisker of one away goal difference when we were beaten 1–0.

CLOUGHIE DROPS A CLANGER

At the start of the 1979/80 season, Cloughie dropped a right clanger that financially cost the club dearly.

Before every season begins, although the players are on different basic pay, they have the same bonuses. Cloughie was having a good old drink up with us one night and we got round to trying to work out how many points we'd need to win the league the following season. We calculated we'd need 50 points to win and so he said, 'For every point you get over 47, you will be paid £1,000.'

Well, we hit 54, which normally would have clinched the title, but, as it happened, Liverpool played brilliantly that season and notched up a fantastic 60 points.

We therefore finished second but the club still had to shell out £7,000 a piece extra as the deal had been signed and sealed. This is a true story – ask any of the other lads. We were well chuffed.

CLOUGHIE ON THE WAR PATH

If we were playing badly or losing a match we should be winning, we would get a terrible roasting from Cloughie at half-time. Oh! The yelling and shouting was ear-splitting. It was horrible.

Robbo had the right idea; he used to disappear into a loo and light up a cigarette. He thought he was doing it in secret but the dozy bugger didn't realise the smoke was curling up over the top of the door. As the rest of us had our ears trained to what Cloughie was ranting and raving about, our eyes would be watching the rising smoke. Surprisingly, this little distraction would have a calming effect on the lecture and Cloughie would more often than not shrug his shoulders and say, 'Let him get away with it.'

I was always getting fined, and one time Robbo and I got into hot water together that ended up in another huge fine. We were in Switzerland and fancied going out for a beer (nothing new there) which was not allowed. So we climbed down a drainpipe and legged it to the nearest pub.

Of course, we got caught – as we usually did – and were fined a whole bloody week's wages. A bit strong, we thought.

You've heard how personal Cloughie could get. If he didn't like you, he told you. Now, I know just how much he admired Robbo. He has often spoken out about his winger's incredible skills. But he was less than kind when it came to personal issues. I guess you could say he was a rude but funny bugger. Of Robbo, he said, 'John Robertson was a very unattractive young man. If one day I felt a bit off colour, I would sit next to him. I was bloody Errol Flynn compared to John, but give him a ball and a yard of grass and he was an artist; the Picasso in our game.'

He also reckoned he turned Robbo from an overweight and average player into an international superstar. I'm not sure he can take *all* the credit for Robbo's rise to superstar but he certainly had a hand in it.

I categorically disagree with the 'unattractive' part of Cloughie's observations. If he reckons Robbo is ugly, I'm not sure where that leaves me! I know he once referred to me as 'A Brick Wall', and I've even read a description of me in his autobiography *Walking On Water* – I think words beginning with 'L' come to mind, like 'lump' or 'lumbering'. But, hey, enough of the derogatory statements, I think Robbo and I, in our youth, were fucking handsome!

Despite us winning silverware and giving our utmost to the club, it was not all hearts and flowers in the Nottingham camp. Cloughie and I were always clashing about something or other, and, if it wasn't us two at loggerheads, it was him and Martin O'Neill, or one of the others who had the balls to stand up to him. As I said, he quite rightly had a reputation of being a bigheaded loudmouth, and he *always* had to have the last word. He insisted on dominating his players, and, well, I think you know me well enough by now to know I wasn't prepared to allow him to dominate me. I had never been controlled, and I never would be.

Oh! The rows – they went on and on.

If I'm honest, I got off on the wrong foot with Clough from the beginning. But the crunch came between us over what was referred to in the press as 'The Great Blazer Row'. It happened the morning after Forest beat AEK Athens in the 1978/79 European Cup second-round match in Greece.

I'm positive to this day that no instruction was given to me to wear my club blazer to travel home, but when I boarded the coach for the airport everyone except for me – that's 15 out of 16 players – was wearing the club uniform of blue blazer and grey slacks. I was in jeans, a casual jacket and open-neck shirt.

'Why are you the odd one out?' Clough was not a happy bunny.

But I told him, 'Nobody – but nobody – has told me anything different.' I wouldn't have had a problem wearing the club uniform. I was proud to wear it, but I honestly never heard this was what was required.

'Go and change immediately,' he said.

'I can't. My clothes are packed away in my case which has already been loaded on to the coach.'

Nothing more was said till the next day when Clough handed me a fine known as a 'Red Tree' because it was given to you in an envelope on which Forest's motif of a red tree is printed.

I was confused. 'What's this all about?'

'Don't open it till you get home.'

But, being me, I tore into the envelope straight away to find I'd been fined £100 for breach of club discipline. 'I'm not paying this,' I spat. 'I had *not* been instructed I had to wear the uniform.'

'That, Lloydie, has just cost you another £100.'

'OK, let's jump straight to £500, 'cos I've still got plenty to say.' I was growling by now.

This was the trait in me that added fuel to Cloughie's fire. He simply *had* to have the last word – but so did I. It was back in my schoolboy days when this stubbornness kicked in – so it was difficult, if not impossible, to break the deeply ingrained habit.

'Then £500 it is,' he said. Then he cruelly scrubbed my name off the team sheet.

That brought the old red mist down, I can tell you. Telling me I couldn't play was a bridge too far. So I stormed off to see him the day after the match when I'd sat miserably on the bench determined to ask for a transfer (déjà vu, or what!). But Clough was away on one of his many Spanish holidays so instead I came face to face with Peter Taylor and the chairman Stuart Dryden.

These more mild-mannered men were an easier force to deal with and this had the result of calming me down. It wasn't too long before we were managing to discuss things reasonably. They didn't want me to put in for a transfer and a compromise was struck, whereupon I paid the original £100 fine. The whole unfortunate issue blew over eventually, but this example of two similar characters clashing highlights just why Clough and I would never have been mates.

Neither of us was the kind of man who would budge an inch. But I have to say, I learned a valuable lesson from the blazer row and was never much bother after that – even though he provoked me time and time again. I guess I learned to deal better with the red mist when it came down.

He told me straight one day. 'I don't like you.' And he let me know during a team talk and therefore in front of a dressing room full of Forest players.

I'd been out of action for a while with a broken foot, and during this time he brought in another centre-half, David Needham. David and I just happened to be sitting next to each other when he turned to David and said, 'I don't understand you, David. Why do you keep letting him [me] get in the team?'

David and I looked at each other, wondering what verbal abuse was coming next.

Clough went on, 'To start with, you've got a big advantage over Lloyd. I like you and I don't like him.'

There was complete silence in the room. You could've heard a pin drop as everyone wondered where this was going.

Clough addressed David: 'David, you've done ever so well since I bought you from Queens Park Rangers, and I can't fault you. You are a lovely man. If my daughter was looking for a man to bring home to introduce to marry, you'd be that man. You're that nice, and the reason why you're not in the team.' Then he pointed to me and finished his speech by saying, 'You're not a fucking bastard like him.'

He was a bit of a psychologist was Cloughie. He played the reverse psychology game so well in order to get what he wanted.

At first I wanted to fly at him, but then I realised he had actually given me a compliment – well, as far as being a footballer was concerned. It lifted me no end. I had been feeling anxious about my place in the team, as I had broken my foot in two places and knew only too well what injuries can do to your career. They can end it overnight. I had stupidly tried to get fit and back in the side too quickly which set me back further. Yes, I can honestly say I was panicking.

David Needham, being slightly younger than me, and playing well, made me nervous. As did the fact that we had beaten Manchester United in a massive 4–0 win, and then Bury away in something like a 7–1 victory, with David Needham in the side on both occasions.

However much Cloughie and I clashed, when that team sheet went up on the Friday, it was always No.5 Lloyd. Whatever he thought of me personally, he respected me for my ability and attitude on the pitch. And I respected him for the manager he was.

Tactically, I thought he was crap. His skill lay in buying a group of players who all knew their jobs and then letting them get on with it. He never coached in the true sense of the word either. But this was his way and, fuck, his way worked.

He prepared us identically each week. It didn't matter who we were playing – the preparation was always the same.

He didn't care about the opposition; it could be Manchester United or Scunthorpe, the training and instructions never changed. He told us that if we played our best and played as a team we could beat anyone. The key to winning was holding our own position and never coming out of it. The ball would come to us in due time and we had to be there when it came. In his book marking an opponent wasn't necessary.

Fitness was all important and we relied a lot on muscle memory. As I said, Cloughie built up his team carefully by choosing characters that, collectively, would get the job done. Needless to say, we all played well together. It was us against them. With tough bastards in midfield as well as at the back, and Shilton in goal, we were a hard team to score against. Just one goal from Tony Woodcock and a 1–0 win would be in the bag.

CHAPTER 17

ENGLAND RECALL

WALES V ENGLAND, Home Championship, 17 May 1980
We lost 4–1 to the Welsh for the first time since 1955 – a very
long time as I was only seven years old and food rations weren't
long over then!

AS YOU CAN see by the date, I had to wait a full eight years for my
next call-up. By now I was a senior player and a Nottingham Forest
legend with lots of trophies and medals to my name. Cloughie was
my manager and, to be honest, although I was coming towards the
end of my playing career, I was still playing solid games for Forest.
The England manager of this era was Ron Greenwood, and the
squad players were an awesome bunch, but Greenwood must have
been watching me closely and thought I was up for the job.

I started alongside the man whom I had had some torrid
moments at Liverpool – one Phil Thompson. Ray Clemence was in
goal, while Phil Neal and Trevor Cherry made up the rest of the

defence. Then there was Glen Hoddle and Trevor Brooking in the middle of the field with Ray Kennedy (at that time at Liverpool), Manchester United's Stevie Coppell and Paul Mariner of Ipswich up front with West Brom striker Peter Barnes. It shows the kind of class that was on the pitch – besides me of course – when we had the likes of Kenny Sansom (then at Crystal Palace but soon to move to Arsenal) on the bench when the whistle blew to signal the beginning of what was to be a disaster for England and a personal nightmare for Lloydie!

Just as when I had started my international career, I found myself in a much changed side, which is always a minus, and, although we began well, it soon went downhill fast.

Some reports said that this was England's worst ever performances, but I think that is an unfair comment, as the Welsh side played well. In my opinion, they deserved a victory not only because of our mistakes but also because of their spirit and determination.

We actually took the lead after just 15 minutes when Trevor Cherry bombed down the left wing and crossed to Peter Barnes in the centre, who in turn fired a shot which Paul Mariner picked up and netted. Thomas came back for the Welsh and scored a goal from close range

Inspired by their comeback, they started to attack our goal furiously. Much to my horror, I then had a nightmare of a game in every sense possible. The only thing that could have been any worse would have been for me to be red-carded – though that might even have been a relief!

Phil Neal got injured next and on came Kenny Sansom to slot into the left-back position, while Trevor Cherry went over to the right. Then there I was stuck in the centre in between Kenny and Trevor and, to be honest, I was suddenly all over the place. Swansea's

Robbie James, who was their star player and had set up the first goal, kept pulling me out of position and it took about half an hour of this hellish match for Wales to take the lead. James flew around the right of me and, like a bat out of hell, sped forward and chipped an immaculate pass over to Ian Walsh, who seemed to take off into orbit where, from a great height, he headed the ball past Ray Clemence.

I was as mad as I could have been — and, believe me, that is extremely mad — and began stomping around making a nuisance of myself, earning a booking in the process. But we battled on and on, and Barnes came agonisingly close to scoring. Unfortunately, one of their defenders got in the damn way to send it off target.

Poor old Glen Hoddle must have really got the hump because he was playing out of his skin, while defensively we were all pretty shit. By contrast, Wales's James was inspired, as was Joey Jones, and it was 66 minutes exactly when Wales put their fourth goal in the back of the net; I wanted to curl up and die. There were another few minutes of mayhem in which the normally mild-mannered Trevor Brooking tried unsuccessfully to bring down Giles — I would have clattered the bastard — who ran hell for leather at the goal. Phil Thompson managed to stop him in his tracks; the problem was, instead of clearing the ball, Phil scored an own goal. We were humiliated and devastated, and I was still as mad as a hatter — barking, growling and behaving like a hard nut while feeling like mush inside.

Then I injured my ankle, which almost kept me out the European Cup Final for Forest. I should have saved myself the trouble and stamped on it myself — though my injury might have been far worse if I had!

If I was to tell you this was my last game for my country, would you be surprised? No, I didn't think so.. While Wales rejoiced (just as Northern Ireland had done eight years before on their record-winning game), we glumly returned to our dressing room for the bollocking we knew we deserved.

As for me, I knew it was game over as far as my international career went. The squad went on to the European Championships that year in Italy, and needless to say I wasn't in it. Oh, the memory hurts almost as much all these years on.

Yet my overriding memories of my England career are brilliant. Each and every squad I played with was full of colourful characters that I had got to know very well during league matches. There was always something going on and the entertainment value was outstanding. Bobby Moore, Alan Ball, Mike Summerbee, Francis Lee, Geoff Hurst and, of course, the crazy Rodney Marsh were fantastic mates. You had to have your wits about you at all times or they would take the piss unmercifully, but saying that they also made the younger internationals feel at home and I thoroughly enjoyed their company, as well as learning an awful lot from them.

CHAPTER 18

THE END OF THE GLORY DAYS

THE END OF my days as a Forest player were frustrating. I felt – well, many of us felt – that Clough was getting rid of players and breaking up the team too early. We had so much more left in us. I knew that, as far as I was concerned, I had at least one more season left in me. I now knew how Bill Shankly felt when, in *his* playing days, he too felt they had been brought to a premature end. But Cloughie was impulsive, and it struck me he didn't give decisions enough thought – and, of course, he had the last word. Bastard.

I was giving my future a hell of a lot of thought. I wanted to stay in the world of football. I felt I had a lot more to give to the game, and the more I asked myself what I wanted, the more I realised I'd like to be a player-manager.

The relationship between Clough and me couldn't have been worse. 'Oh, just sort out my contract and I'll fuck off,' I sighed one day, when I could take no more. 'I'm going to be a player-manager.'

Cunning Clough's response was nothing short of what I had

come to expect from him. 'I know, I'll do a big spread in the *Sun* concentrating on the breaking up of the team, and I'll say that I will predict Larry Lloyd will become a great manager.'

I had been one of the heroes of Nottingham Forest's two European Cup campaigns, and been part of the phenomenal side that grasped an immense victory that took us from the Second Division to the First – then we raced up the league to win it in the next season. Those are amazing feats.

Our team retained the European Cup against Hamburg and it seemed absolutely nuts for us to be disbanded; we felt as if we were still in our prime, and had lots more to give.

Things might have changed now, what with modern training regimes, dietary advice and the like, which allow players to stay match fit well into their thirties, but, when a player hit the age of 30 back then, Cloughie would start looking for replacements. I was 32 when he called me into his office and gave me the bad news.

'Larry, I'll be straight down the line with you because I know that's how you want me to deal with you, and I don't intend for you to be my number-one centre-half next season.'

'You're fucking kidding, aren't you?' I couldn't believe my ears.

'I'm looking for a younger man.'

'But I've still got 18 months left on my contract.'

'I don't think you really want to be a reserve player.'

The bastard had got me. He knew I had been thinking about going into management, so he seduced me by saying, 'I'll help you out. I'll tell the press what a great player-manager you would make.'

Frank Clark had already gone, Archie went just before me, and Kenny went just after me. The following season, Garry Birtles went to Manchester United, Ian Bowyer to Sunderland and Martin O'Neill to Norwich City. That, as they say, was that! Game over for the Glory Boys.

My days playing in the same team as my mate John Robertson were over – more sadness! I have no hesitation in saying that little fat bastard was a magician. He was slower than me physically, but, because his brain was quicker than anybody else's, he had the first two yards on anybody.

If he were to race 20 players from the corner flag to the halfway line, he'd be last. He was the slowest by far, but when it came to it he had the extra two yards. He would put his fat arse one way and the opposition would go that way – so would the crowd of 50,000 that were watching. He would be the only one who went the other way with the ball stuck firmly to his feet. As I said before, the guy was both a gentleman and a genius.

It was a sad day when I left. Yes, I was excited about my future venture but it really was one of the saddest days of my life. I tell you what else was bloody sad – Clough replaced me with Willy Young.

Now, Willy was a solid, steady player, but he was also my age. What a liberty!

So clever old Cloughie, who just *had* to get his own way, kept his promise, and told the press, 'The time is right for Larry to move on, and we certainly won't stand in his way. He has ambitions to go into management and, if a player-manager job comes up, we won't object to him leaving. I'm certain he will do a fantastic job for someone… and I mean off the field as well as on it. He is keen to start afresh. When he came to us, his career was on the rocks but so was this club. He has made a major contribution to putting us where we are today. It's been a dual thing – we've been good for Larry Lloyd and he's been good for Nottingham Forest.'

At least he was spot on with his summing up of our union.

In the five years I was with Forest, we achieved so much. The highlight was winning back-to-back European Cups – a feat no other club has managed, except Liverpool. In the 1977/78 season, we equalled the all-time record for the least number of goals conceded, which was 24, and I had been a part of that defence. We went 42 league games without defeat, holding the record for 25 years, until Arsenal broke it.

Given these incredible results, I honestly don't think we were given the accolades we deserved. I also believe, had we been Manchester United, or one of the big London clubs, the media would have made much more fuss of us.

It has been said that I am one of the most underrated players of my time; if that is true, then Nottingham Forest must also rank amongst the most underrated clubs. In my mind we have both been underrated.

END OF CLOUGHIE AND TAYLOR

When Brian Clough passed away at the age of 69 on 20 September 2004, it was a sad day for football. Although I've slagged Old Big 'Ed off a bit, I have to concede that the man was a bloody genius who loved his football and did more for the club than Nottingham Forest can ever thank him for. I totally appreciated him as a manager.

Clough, like me and many other footballers who have made the big time, was raised in a safe and secure home with bundles of love and praise. I believe that, when a child is raised in this type of environment, they can flourish and grow into a man who is capable of reaching his potential.

He claimed to be 'the thick boy who was made head boy'. He excelled at all sports, especially football.

After doing his national service and working for ICI, he was signed as a junior with Middlesbrough FC in 1955 and this is where he first met Peter Taylor who was the reserve-team goalkeeper. They quickly became friends, and the most famous and successful double act in English football was born.

Clough is famous for his managerial skills, but not too many people outside the Midlands realise just what a great player he was. While playing for Middlesbrough, he scored 204 goals in 222 appearances, and then went on to Sunderland where he scored 63 in 74 games, until a bad knee injury at Roker Park on Boxing Day 1962 cut short his remarkable record-breaking playing career. He also won two full England caps.

His career in football management began at Hartlepool United, and he moved to Derby with his family in June 1962 when he took on the management job at Derby County. They won the Second Division title and were promoted to what was in effect the top league at that time. Derby went on to become league champions in 1971/72 (while I was at Liverpool, playing against the buggers) and the following year he took them to the semi-finals of the European Cup.

He made the following statement about walking out on Derby after a much publicised boardroom row: 'It was the greatest mistake I ever made in football.'

Rather like my biggest mistake when I demanded a transfer from Liverpool! No wonder the two of us clashed – two big hotheads who would never back down. But our backgrounds and personalities also ensured we communicated at the highest levels and the job got done.

In the years prior to his death, he took a swipe at 'player power', and said that he was despairing of English football. He gave an interview to the *Sun*, telling them that a player's ambition should start with winning a game. 'I gave my players a version of the same message at ten to three every Saturday afternoon: I would shoot my granny right now for three points this afternoon. They knew how important it was to give everything in the cause of victory. Every time. That's why my granny enjoyed more lives than my cat.'

I always knew Cloughie was a bigger bastard than me; at least I only ever admitted to the notion I'd kick *my* granny!

Martin O'Neill, Robbo and I have spent so many great evenings chatting about our old boss and his outspoken manner. Martin told us about how Cloughie finished in the top three of an online poll to elect Nottingham's first 'virtual' MP. In the first and second places were Robin Hood and actress Su Pollard.

Peter was a better judge of a player than Cloughie; having an uncanny knack of spotting talent, he would go out and find the player and then send Clough out to reel him in. Clough knew he was the front man, and Peter was happy to be the man in the background. This arrangement suited their personalities perfectly. Taylor has said, 'We just gelled together, we filled in the gaps.'

In June 1967, both of them joined Derby County who were promoted to the First Division two years later. Cloughie has made no secret about his regret about leaving Derby – but, hey, if I hadn't left Liverpool and he hadn't left Derby, we would never have had those glory years at Nottingham Forest.

Next they went on to Brighton together, but nine months later Clough was kind of 'reeled in' by Leeds United, where he took over from Don Revie.

After Leeds sacked him, he went to Nottingham Forest, and, needless to say, although Peter Taylor had made lots of noises about wanting to stay on the south coast where his family were enjoying living by the sea, it wasn't long before they were back together doing their double act. I entered their awesome sphere soon afterwards.

Cloughie said in his autobiography *Walking On Water* that he and Peter Taylor 'dragged in new recruits from all corners, nooks and crannies and the occasional dog track', and I was one of those recruits.

Clough said, 'Larry Lloyd came from Coventry where he seemed to have disappeared after managing to earn an England cap or two while he was at Liverpool.' Hmm... put like that, I realise how much I should be grateful to him for saving me.

It was Peter Taylor and Cloughie who came up with the winning formula which consisted of one shit-hot goalkeeper, two powerful centre-halves and one brilliant centre-forward. These were the backbone and framework – the absolute skeleton of any side.

If Cloughie had any favourites, I'd say they would have been my best mate Robbo and Martin O'Neill, even though he clashed with Martin and got fed up with Martin threatening to pack up football and go back to university every time he was left out of the side. One day, he told Martin he'd already packed his bags and had paid his ticket home – that shut Martin up on that score.

It was never made obvious, but I picked up on it, and would also agree that these are two extraordinary men.

I think Cloughie, before he died, was proud of how well Martin and Robbo were working together in management, and took some credit for this. In his autobiography he described them as: 'Martin O'Neill and John Robertson – the academic and the scruff – the Irishman and the Scotsman – chalk and cheese – just like Taylor and me.'

Sadly, the great duo of Clough and Taylor came to a bitter end and it was all over my mate Robbo. It concerned a dispute over Robbo's transfer from Forest to Derby in May 1983. They stopped talking and never made it up, which was sad because Peter died a premature death while on holiday in Majorca. He was only 62 years old. Cloughie went to the funeral, and he also dedicated his 1994 autobiography to him. I could only deduce from this that Clough still cared deeply for the man he spent the best part of his life with.

CHAPTER 19

SUE, YOLANDA AND DAMIAN

YOLANDA WAS TEN and Damian two years younger when Sue and I faced another crossroads in our life. Should we stay in Nottingham, a city we had grown to love, or should be move to Wigan, where I was to be player-manager? It was basically down to Sue, as the children were getting older now and all sorts of things had to be taken into consideration.

Don't forget that Sue had always been extremely accommodating – moving around the country to help satisfy her ambitious husband's needs. Was this going to prove to be one move too many? She wanted to play it by ear, to see how I coped with the travelling, and how she and the children found four days a week without their 'Pop'.

I should have thought Sue would be glad of the space; after all, I was getting bigger by the day!

Wigan had been quick off the mark to make me an offer when they learned of the player-manager direction I had chosen. So,

175

overnight I went from one of the oldest players in the First Division, to the youngest manager in the football league.

Sue had jumped at moving to Liverpool when we were first married, and she didn't complain about going to Coventry. In fact she was quite happy there in our pretty house in the country, but she'd admitted she had begun to feel as if she was in a prison.

'I've realised, Larry,' she confessed to me one day, 'that houses are just bricks and mortar. It's where you are and who you are with that really matters.'

So when we'd moved from our isolated village near Coventry to Nottingham, we'd chosen very carefully, and settled into friendly West Bridgford.

Sue loved the shopping precinct in Nottingham, the Exchange Arcade. She loved to roam around the shops, and one of her first impressions of the city had been how clean it was; it really felt pretty upmarket.

Sue was a great mum, and I think she got her priorities right most of the time. If there was a choice between housework or a day out with the kids, a day out would win every time. If it was sunny, she would ignore the ironing and sunbathe. The dusting was always on the waiting list – and why not!

One plus about a decision to move to Wigan was that we wouldn't be far from all the friends we'd made in Liverpool. They kept ringing us up and asking when we were going to move back, but we really couldn't decide. And we felt it best not to move if we weren't certain.

The children were settled too – Nottingham had indeed become home.

My kids had grown up with a famous dad, and I didn't think it had fazed them at all, although, later on, when we sat and talked about their childhood they had plenty to say, some good and some not so good.

Yolanda has said she missed me 'horribly' when I was in hospital with my back injury. She sent me this sweet little note that said, 'Dear Dade Mummy dussnt luff us anymore. Please come home soon!'

She also remembers that the sixties song 'Concrete and Clay', by Unit 4+2, was playing on the car radio as we drove home. She was delighted about this because she knew it was my favourite. Yolanda's right – I loved that song. We were talking just the other day and she told me she still gets a lump in her throat if she hears the song.

'Dade,' she said (she alternates between Pop and Dade), 'I didn't really understand the seriousness of your operation, but I must have picked something up unconsciously, because I was really upset and scared. I was just so happy when you came back home.'

It brings a lump to my throat as I write this, I can tell you.

Damian once queued up for my autograph along with his mates. He said it was more exciting than being at home with me! Kids! I had always found the fame thing – the whole celebrity phenomenon – a strange affair.

John Robertson was a regular visitor at our house, and Yolanda and Damian were very fond of him. When it came to voting for 'Nottingham Forest Player of The Year', they were all for voting for Uncle John, until their mum told them they should be supporting their dad, which actually surprised me, as Sue was always one to try to play the fame thing down to the children. She was eager for them to develop personalities of their own and not live in the shadow of a big old bastard like me.

Robbo had two daughters of his own, Elizabeth and Jessica; tragically, Jessica died when she was just 13. Robbo was naturally devastated.

John and both his first and second wives were wonderful with Yolanda and Damian. We all got on famously, like one big family. Weddings, funerals, any social event saw us all together.

Yolanda says me and Robbo are like one huge mutual appreciation society. She commented once, 'I know about every kick in every match you two have played in together.'

Christ, we must have been boring buggers to have to listen to at times!

When I went away on a tour, my homecoming was always special. The kids were all over me like a rash whenever I returned.

We have often sat and chatted about their childhood years, and what it was like having a professional footballer for a father. Yolanda and Damian are very different characters. I used to think that Damian was more sensitive than his older sister, but he says she was simply better at hiding her insecurities behind a strong mask.

One thing I know Damian did find annoying was being referred to at school as 'Little Larry'. The headmaster was always talking about my triumphs and talent and I think many assumed – quite wrongly – that Damian would want to follow in my footsteps, but, as I said, they were encouraged to be themselves rather than an extension of my achievements. I always refer to them as 'my rocks', but, according to Yolanda, I have been my kids' rock too. So that can't be bad.

I remember Yolanda saying that she thought both me and her mum were 'cool' parents. I suppose we were. We had them when we were young, and our lifestyle was exciting. Sue was a beauty, and I suppose I wasn't too bad looking either with my long dark sideburns and tall muscular body. Some have likened me to the late George Best, although my modesty wouldn't allow me to take things that far!

SUE, YOLANDA AND DAMIAN

Sue and I had married in 1969 when I was a young man with a dream and she was a student nurse also full of hope for a career. The divorce, when it came, was a crushing blow to all of us. We had been married 17 long happy years. Our children, like all children who watch their parents' love for each other dissolve in front of their eyes, were deeply affected. Yolanda became a punk, and, although she claimed it was normal to wear purple lipstick and spike her hair, I begged to differ.

Damian, to this day, still has issues with his mother that need resolving. Sue chose to emigrate to Australia when, in my opinion, he was too young. In my opinion, that young boy still needed his mum around.

Sue and I had had a wonderful marriage, and there was much 'shall we, shan't we' before we actually split.

I had always been faithful to Sue. I am a 'one girl at a time' kind of guy – that's just how I am. I can flirt like the rest, but I could never do the dirty. It's not my style. Anyway, she'd have cut my bollocks off if she'd ever caught me playing away off the pitch.

Seriously, we were both faithful to each other, and I am proud of that. I think that we had so much respect for each other as human beings that to betray one another would have been awful.

Everybody who knew us was totally shocked when we told them we were getting divorced. 'Why? You are so good together,' they said.

Yet, as time went on and our lifestyles changed, we did what many couples do – we drifted apart, each lost in our own particular needs.

Ironically, life after football should have seen us doing more things together, but that didn't happen. Perhaps all the time I had spent working away had given us the opportunity to enjoy our own company and grow into very different people.

We had nothing in common any more. Sue was a livewire and would love to go out on Sundays sightseeing and suchlike. I, on the other hand, loved to take it easy at home with the Sunday papers and a roast dinner. She wanted to walk in the Derbyshire hills and I was content to down a pint at the local pub.

I remember her mother died around this time, and the loss hit her hard. Maybe she re-evaluated her life and decided she wanted to live a little more – in her world, rather than mine. She said she wanted to 'find herself'. How many times do we hear that old chestnut? But I said, 'I found you. You're here with me.' But I guess I was no longer enough. Sue was about to spread her wings.

Looking back, we must have been collecting stress points all along the way. Moving house and towns so many times, and living with all that upheaval. We married at the age of 20 and, although she was ambitious in her own way, she had put her career on hold to live life in the shadows of a professional footballer, as well as to be a mum.

As far as divorces go, it was a 'nice' divorce. Well, actually, not *so* nice! I can remember as clearly as if it was yesterday, when we sat in our cosy kitchen at our long table that had witnessed many happy family meals, and she said, 'We must have closure, Larry.'

The kids were at school so we were alone when we spoke of dividing everything equally. Tackling the issues of bank accounts and savings investments, we were determined to be fair.

That was, until I asked my helpful pal John Robertson if he knew of a good solicitor for Sue. Bad mistake. He came up with this shit-hot divorce lawyer in Nottingham who advised her she was entitled to more. *What... and leave me with nothing? How does that work?* Well, I had another quick word in my mate's ear, and he in turn had a word in this solicitor's ear. It all got a bit naughty for a while, but thankfully everything got sorted in the end.

SUE, YOLANDA AND DAMIAN

Honestly, sometimes these solicitors cause more trouble than they're worth. Here we were, a couple who had met as kids in the school yard and later lost their virginity together, had taken marriage vows, experienced the magic of our children's births, and were now going our own way in the world. How could we be arguing over sodding money while some stranger acted as mediator, telling us how to split our finances? Sometimes I think the world has gone totally mad.

Yolanda, Damian and I have often spoken about when their mother and I split up. They said it was a horrible time for them. After an idyllic childhood, to watch their parents split up and lead separate lives was devastating.

Yolanda said, 'Suddenly you both had other things and other people on your minds. We were no longer living in a secure and safe home.' She was right; new relationships were looming, and when Yolanda added, 'Nothing was ever the same again,' I knew she was right and how tough that must have been for two young kids going through puberty.

We had decided to share custody of Yolanda and Damian, although this didn't quite go to plan. They both ended up living with me in my house in Nottingham. First Yolanda arrived on the doorstep with her suitcase. 'Can I come and live with you, Pop?' And Damian wasn't far behind. I was as happy as Larry with this development, I can tell you.

So, there I was, in my mid-thirties having to chat a bird up, and what a minefield *that* turned out to be.

During the ten years between marriages to Sue and my second wife Debbie, I dated several women, and ran away from more than I can remember. I found the new and liberated women who got drunk and then suggested sex a real turn-off. How can you go to bed and have sex before you've even had a date? It's nuts, and very wrong – isn't it? I was confused. What the hell had happened to romance since I had last dated a girl in the 1960s?

I wanted to romance a girl. That was all I knew. Basic manners I'd been taught as a boy didn't seem to mean jack shit any more. If you opened a door for a woman, she looked at you as if you'd grown two heads. Holding hands wasn't 'cool' and, as for looping your arm around their shoulders and expecting them to hug you round your waist, that was a definite no-no. Now they would just walk along next to you swinging their designer handbags and swigging from a bottle of beer with a wedge of lemon or lime stuck in the top, and I would look on in wonderment.

This new breed was everywhere. All these dominant women asking, 'D'you wanna fuck?'

I was terrified. I might have been a hard and tough central defender but, where the opposite sex was concerned, I found it impossible to defend myself.

One young lady wanted to take me home and have her way with me on a waterbed. *Waterbed!!* There would have been a major tsunami in Nottingham.

I learned a hell of a lot about the 'Mars and Venus' way of looking at a relationship. We were from different planets all right. Don't get me wrong – I *like* women, I simply don't *understand* them.

Sue and I could chat for hours, but these new-age women didn't seem to think having an intelligent chat was a worthwhile pastime. Had there been a 'gender quake' throughout the seventies and eighties? And, if so, just why was this? The feminist movement had occurred decades ago, hadn't it? I had so many questions, but not the sniff of an answer resided in my testosterone-loaded brain.

Perhaps this was the result of the liberation of the birth pill during the sixties? That's what some people were telling me. They said women had more choices now, and this was because they were suddenly earning good wages of their own. Now, I have nothing against equality, nothing whatsoever. If a woman works hard, she is as entitled as any man to reap the rewards of her efforts. My own daughter is one such woman.

But I have come to the conclusion that the balance has shifted too far and now men are confused, while women are shooting themselves in the foot with their new powers.

One girl said to me, 'Why would I want to be with you? I probably earn more money in a week than you do in a month.' She went on to tell me she could only ever be with a man who earned more than she did. I felt like a right twat, and the shit just kept on coming; so much so that an initial feeling of confusion led to a far deeper sense of inadequacy. Paranoia set in and I began to wonder whether they were purposely trying to cut my balls off.

But, when I started asking around, I was relieved to hear that I was not alone in my way of thinking. Other divorced and separated men were coming across similar scenarios.

One of my mates fell in love with the voice of a woman over the phone. He had called a company about purchasing something and he said the woman on the other end of the line had 'the sexiest voice ever'. After chatting for a while, he asked her on a date, and they agreed to meet outside a famous department store.

Being a gentleman, he arrived early, eagerly awaiting his princess. When she showed up, she was wearing scuffed high-heeled shoes (and, yes, they were white! Ugh!) and a skirt that barely covered her arse. In her sexy voice, she asked, 'Where are we going?'

My mate had planned on taking his princess with the sexy voice to his favourite upmarket restaurant, but instead he answered, 'The Harvester... is that OK?'

It's not funny. It's tragic. I don't want to be a new-age man. I just want to be a man and I want women to be how they used to be. Pint-swilling women with foul mouths are a turn-off, and no one can tell me any different.

I tell you, that bewildering ten years in the 'women wilderness' was a confusing decade of my attempting to work women out; and, by the time I met and married Debbie, it seems I had learned fuck all.

But my immediate problem when I left Nottingham Forest was focusing on my new player-manager role. Thank God I still had my football.

CHAPTER 20

WIGAN GO 'OOP'!

'With his playing career over, Larry took on the job of manager at Wigan. In his first game in charge, nine of his players managed to find their way into the referee's notebook. During the post-game interview, a reporter asked Larry, who had been famous throughout his career as a very physical, tough, tackling defender, what he had to say about nine of his players getting booked in his first game in charge. Without missing a beat, Larry looked at the reporter and said, "Well, I'm going to have to question the commitment of the other two!"'

THE ABOVE STORY is not only true but is now a question in Trivial Pursuit. I played in a tough physical manner, and managed my men the same way.

I was as 'Happy as Larry' when I joined Fourth Division Wigan. I was 32 years of age and I was about to become player-manager – the first in Wigan's history. I succeeded Ian McNeil who, after five years in the hot seat, was sacked.

I had been a vital part in helping Forest to promotion from the Second Division in 1977, and had figured in all their League and European Cup successes, but now I was ready for a very different challenge.

I had really wanted to take the player-manager route, and it felt rather like the time when Liverpool stepped in and bought me from Bristol Rovers, in that everyone was seeking my services.

Back then, many other teams such as Fulham and even Manchester United had been sniffing around, whereas, now, it could have easily been Millwall or another meaty team I could have been joining. But I was quick to express interest in taking on the Wigan job when I heard about the firing of McNeil.

I had left the City Ground in the knowledge that this was another step in the 'new broom' policy of the Forest management. As I said, many of us had left for pastures new, and I was one of them.

The Wigan fans looked on me as being a battle-hardened international who could bring a more professional approach to the players under his control. They knew I was a fierce competitor with fire still rushing through my veins. I looked on it this way: I had gone from a poacher to gamekeeper. I knew now that it was a case of 'them doing as *I* say' – which was far away from my hot-headed playing days when I was giving management reason to dislike me. The 'Raging Bull' days were now behind me… well, more or less! After all, a leopard can't completely change his spots.

Wigan fans also got very excited about my wealth of experience. Having played for prestigious teams such as Bristol Rovers, Liverpool, Coventry and Nottingham Forest – not to mention, England – they looked to me to do great things for their club. They wanted me to produce a side that would be hard to beat and therefore achieve the promotion they desired so much.

The great bosses I had served under – Fred Ford, Bill Shankly, Sir Alf Ramsey, Gordon Milne and, of course, Brian Clough – had had a huge influence on me. They had all been very different characters. Although I didn't realise it at the time, I had been learning and gradually picking up knowledge. From Fred Ford, I had learned about basic honesty. With him there was no messing around. It was always straight to the point and that is something I have always appreciated. Shanks and Cloughie were vastly different characters but, in some ways, so similar in their approach to winning. Shanks was a football fanatic and I always thought that, had he been a supporter, he would, perhaps, have been a hooligan because he was so uptight about the game. While you could always talk with Clough on a range of subjects, Shanks would always turn the subject back to football within seconds whatever the discussion had started with. All his thoughts were on the game.

When I left Anfield, I thought I was set in my ways but Brian Cough turned all that upside down. His ideas were so different. For example, I'd always been used to having no alcohol after Thursday and being in bed by ten on the eve of a game. I believed in this so firmly that my wife, Sue, used to sleep in a separate room with the kids on a Friday night.

But then, suddenly, I'd found myself going away with Nottingham Forest on a Friday night and coming face to face with six bottles of wine sitting on the table, ready to be consumed with dinner. There were a dozen bottles of champagne consumed the night before our League Cup final against Southampton, and no one went to bed before midnight.

This had been very confusing, and when I was a player I had to find my personal place somewhere between the two extremes. Now I was to become a manager myself, I was acutely conscious of wanting to pitch between those same extremes.

At this time I watched Alan Clarke managing the Leeds side, and felt he was trying to emulate Clough, and it was a mistake because he didn't know him well enough.

Ever the perfectionist, I agonised constantly about doing the right thing by Wigan. I reflected on the type of manger Gordon Milne had been at Coventry. Kindly Gordon guided me through the years between giants Shankly and Cloughie, and in a sense I think I bit the hand that fed me! I had strutted into Highfield Road as though I owned it. Don't forget, I'd arrived at Coventry with a monstrous £240,000 fee hanging round my neck, which was a record for a defender in those days.

I went to Wigan with a new maturity that led me to feel rather ashamed of my behaviour during my time at Coventry. I have come to the conclusion that Gordon was far too nice a man to have a hope in hell of managing me. I would like to emphasise that everything that happened at Coventry was entirely my fault.

You see, I needed a hard bastard like Shankly or Cloughie to bring out the best in me. That was – still is, really – how I am. I got away with murder while at Coventry, but it did me no favours whatsoever. In my defence, my head was simply not on right. I was an idiot back then. Had I said the things I said to Gordon to the other two, they would have murdered me.

Wigan hailed many new beginnings for me – both on and off the pitch. I was a new man in many ways, and this was a great thing for both me and Wigan. I was determined not to tolerate anyone behaving as I did at Coventry. Who did I think I was? It just goes to show how fame and success can go to your head and do terrible things to your mind, making you behave in a bad way!

Shankly, the obsessive manager, would never have allowed this behaviour to materialise, and nor would Bob Paisley, which probably

Above: Hard man, hard game. Liverpool's Steve Heighway discovers just why our defence was nicknamed 'the brick wall' as I plough through him in the first round of the European Cup.

© *Cleva*

Right: European champions! John McGovern, Frank Clark, Gary Birtles (behind me with the hair and moustache) and I hold on tightly to the European Cup we had just won in Munich. There was a sea of red all around, and the Forest fans who had travelled to support us roared and sang, 'Robin Hood, Robin Hood, with his band of men...'

Above: Tony Woodcock and I parade the European Cup round the Olympic Stadium – you couldn't get my hands off the trophy!

© *Action Images*

Below: We also retained the League Cup in 1979 – this time beating Southampton in the final. (*l–r*) John McGovern, Peter Shilton, me, Garry Birtles, Tony Woodcock, David Needham, Frank Clark, John Robertson enjoying a beer and Martin O'Neill.   © *PA Photos*

Above: Defending our European crown in the 1980 final against Hamburg. We went into the game as underdogs as they had Kevin Keegan in the team – but he couldn't get the ball off me here!   *© Cleva*

Below: Retaining the European Cup. We astonished many with our victory but we weren't surprised. Not bad for a supposed 'small' club, eh? (*Back row, l-r*) Martin O'Neill, Ian Bowyer, Viv Anderson, John Robertson, Gary Mills, Kenny Burns; (*front row, l-r*) Frank Gray, Peter Shilton, John McGovern, Garry Birtles, me, Bryn Gunn.   *© PA Photos*

Above left: That's for two European cups, not anything rude! © *PA Photos*

Above right: The glory days – I am voted Player of the Year by the Nottingham Forest fans in the 1979/80 season.

Below: Brian Clough and his Merry Men! (*Back row, l–r*) Peter Shilton, Chris Woods, Ian Bowyer, Frank Clark, John O'Hare, Martin O'Neill, me, Colin Barratt, David Needham, Peter Withe and Cloughie; (*front row, sitting down, l–r*) John 'Robbo' Robertson, Kenny Burns, John McGovern and Archie Gemmill.

                                                 © *Charles A Noble*

Above: A family snap back in '78 – Damian, Sue, Yolanda and me.

© *T. Bailey*

Below: Terry Yorath crunches me – just look at my ankle – as I win my fourth and final England cap against Wales. I had a bloody 'mare!

© *PA Photos*

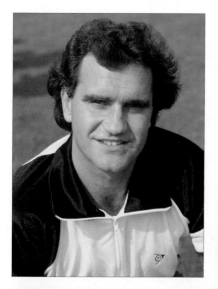

Above left: At Wigan, where I finished my playing days. © *Action Images*

Above right: Yolanda, aged fifteen, in her 'punk' days, my little mum in the middle and Damian in top hat and tails.

Below: My days as a bachelor boy running 'The Stage Door' pub in Nottingham. With me are actor Dennis Waterman and his then wife, the beautiful Rula Lenska.

Above left: Commentating for Century Radio in Nottingham. There's Stan Collymore behind me. © *PA Photos*

Above right: The Hillsborough disaster in 1989. I watched from the stands as the nightmare unfolded – it was pure hell. © *PA Photos*

Below left: Working in the Public Relations office for Forest. © *PA Photos*

Below right: Still got it Lloydie! The waist may be bigger and the hair a little greyer, but I couldn't miss the chance to play for the club I love once more in Mark Crossley's testimonial. © *PA Photos*

It's a wonderful life: With my daughter Yolanda, my son Damian and my granddaughter Georgia.

© Sarah Beretta

had something to do with their finally accepting my transfer request. Then later Cloughie knocked me down to size. Thinking about it now, my dad, although blind, had a way of knocking me into shape and putting me in my place. And as I prepared to take on an authoritative role I missed him dreadfully.

Although I knew there would be difficulties combining playing with managing, I was convinced this was the best way to break into management. And I was right.

It didn't help that I inherited an assistant manager who was an absolute phoney! He had never actually played football at any level to speak of, but simply talked a good talk. In short, he was full of bollocks. Eventually, I just had to let him go. Not the best of starts, but it was soon to get better.

When I joined Wigan, it was the right decision for many reasons, which is why it was a success. Age and maturity were on my side, but I was still young and fit enough to play a great game. I still had stamina, and my defensive play was as hard as ever. I guess I was still solid, strong and a force to be reckoned with on the pitch, but I had also learned how to control myself as a manager and command the respect needed to forge a good working alliance with my players.

Had I transferred any sooner, I would have missed out on a season or two of playing in the First Division. Any longer and it would have been more difficult to get a decent offer to be a player-manager. As it happened my confidence was high, which was an all-important factor.

I took up my new position with an awareness that, for me, management was like bringing up kids. You have to earn respect. You cannot get it by walking in and saying, 'Listen, I demand you respect me!' It doesn't work like that.

One thing I knew for certain was I was not going to rule the roost with an iron fist the way Clough had done with Nottingham

Forest. If Clough were alive today, he would disagree that he worked this way – but he did.

So it was with great ambition and high hopes that my career at Wigan took off. But I soon realised the monumental task ahead of me. One of the first headlines read, 'Slipshod Latics Come to a Sorry End' and I wasn't a Happy Larry at that moment. The text went on to read, 'Wigan Athletic new boy Larry Lloyd was left under no illusions about the task ahead of him at Springfield Park after a depressing 1–0 defeat at the hands of Rochdale.' It went on, 'It could be many players were trying too hard to please their new boss and as a consequence the individual performances of some suffered alarmingly.' My work had begun!

I changed a lot of things in those first few months. There was this terrible thing that the previous manager had done that I put an immediate stop to. Every morning the training kit was thrown into the middle of the room and it was a case of first come, first served. The last man got the ripped and torn rubbish. I thought this was diabolical. I have always thought, 'Your kit is *your* kit, and no one else should wear it.' It's a personal thing.

I instructed the trainer, Kenny Banks, to go out and buy fresh training kit and said each player could have their own till the bloody thing had worn out.

The players' response was: 'Brilliant Boss!'

Then there was a small matter of the training ground and equipment. The ground was a corner of some school playing fields, and we only had one set of goalposts – except we didn't have a net and the frame was a dozen pieces of four-by-four wood crudely nailed together. *What had I left myself in for?*

I rang Peter Taylor at Forest: 'Have you got any spare balls, or kit, or anything else that might help me out?'

'Yes, come on down.'

I got hold of a member of staff and we borrowed this open truck and headed off to the City Ground.

I had a quick coffee and a chat with Peter and Cloughie, then Peter said I should go down to the groundsman's shed where I'd find some bits and bobs.

Well, we rummaged around and found some cones, a few old footballs, nets and several items of kit. Then I saw two portable goal frames folded up in the corner. 'That's handy,' I said to my new man from Wigan. 'Just what we need. Come on, let's load up the truck.' I was well chuffed.

I went and said my goodbyes and thanks, and off we went.

Two days later Peter called me. Shit... he was going mental, swearing and cursing and carrying on alarmingly. 'You've nicked my new goalposts!'

I explained that I thought they were surplus to requirements, and he ranted some more. I told him I had already erected them and my boys were out practising.

'You bastard! You better keep them then.' He was laughing by now. As I said, he's got a good sense of humour. 'Consider them a gift from Nottingham Forest to Wigan.'

Wigan Athletic is a club set in a homely Lancashire town, and I really don't think they knew what hit them when I marched in. I'm a big bloke in every way, and my presence in the corner shop, local pub and the much-loved local football club must have been a little daunting.

To understand the club you need to know a little about Wigan itself.

George Orwell did the identity of Wigan no favours when in 1930 he chose the pier (nothing more than jetty really) on the

Liverpool–Leeds canal as a symbol of squalor. Amazingly, the pier still stands – just! And it is still surrounded by derelict warehouses that once upon a time housed eager employees. But when I joined Wigan Athletic the dole queues were long as were the faces of many troubled locals.

Many people undermine the joy football can bring to people – especially the working classes. Football is tribal and can give a man a sense of belonging, which we all need. I knew then that taking on the job of playing and managing their beloved football team was both a great honour as well as a daunting role. They wanted their team to go 'oop' as they say in that neck of the woods – oop from the Fourth Division to the Third.

Wigan has always been a rugby football town, but that didn't mean soccer wasn't important as well. No one wanted success more than the then Wigan Athletic director John Farrimond, who at the age of 69 was the club's most enduring fan.

Wigan Borough had been elected to the Football League back in 1921, and Farrimond was there to witness this great event. 'It was a cold day and I remember my father bought me a red and white scarf – those were Wigan Borough's colours,' he said.

The team struggled on for ten years when, bust, they gave up the ghost and abandoned their schedule – a decision that didn't go down too well, and rumour was the league never forgave Wigan. It took Wigan Athletic 35 applications before they were reaccepted, and Farrimond allegedly wore out the red carpet at Café Royal every year when the League met.

It's quite incredible that it wasn't until 1978 that they were readmitted – that's one hell of a lot of trying! And I was well aware of the expectations of Wigan Athletic when I took on the job in April 1981.

Freddie Pye, the dynamic scrap merchant chairman, had set the ball rolling for success. He knew what he wanted. Bobby Charlton was the showpiece director, and then there was me, the ex-England, Liverpool and Nottingham Forest legend. We were quite some team.

That said, it was some culture shock for me. One minute I was in Tokyo playing with Forest against Nacional of Uruguay in front of 90,000, playing for the World Club Cup title and two weeks later I was playing against Rochdale in front of 6,000. I had come full-circle back to an audience of a similar size to Bristol Rovers. Incidentally, we lost to Rochdale, and for one fleeting moment I thought perhaps I should have stayed on my bum at Nottingham. But it really was just a fleeting moment. After the shock defeat against Rochdale, I worked like a Trojan, studying the vagaries of the Fourth Division, managing, playing and giving it all so much of my energy.

In a sense, that defeat by Rochdale heralded the beginning of a fairytale that many didn't see coming. I was untried and inexperienced in football management, and some critics back in Bristol said I chose to go to Wigan instead of Millwall because I was a coward – that was bollocks. There were plenty of people back then who would have loved to see me fall flat on my face. But they underestimated old Lloydie's ambitious nature. I had had a brilliant career as a player and now I was determined to be the best manager I could be. I went into management hungry for success, and once I tasted the delicacy I became even hungrier. I became obsessed with taking Wigan into the Third Division. I realised my previous managers had given me so much more than simply being my boss while I played the game – they had also been brilliant mentors that gave me the edge as a good manager. I think the greatest things I learned at my two biggest clubs, Liverpool and Nottingham Forest, were discipline and organisation. Although players tend to rebel against both, deep down they respect them.

While at Wigan I was often compared with Cloughie, and I guess I did have some similar traits. As the time went on during that first season, I *did* feel confident, and at times I'm sure I came across as arrogant. I think this was because I knew my football and how to get the best out of my players. I also wanted to give Freddie Pye credit for the way he backed me when I chose to sign Eamon O'Keefe from Everton. He had every right to laugh in my face when I asked for £65,000 to buy him. There was a lot of criticism and some branded me a spendthrift, but Freddie Pye helped me sign the Evertonian.

When I left Nottingham to go to Wigan, I took a massive wage cut and went back to earnings I had five years before, but there was something much more important going on – I had the smell of success in my nose again, and I followed that smell all the way to the Third Division.

The report in the newspaper said it all. 'Larry Lloyd is a maestro… that's the opinion of his players. The 34-year-old player came in for a lot of credit for Latics' promotion success. Striker Les Bradd said, "His personality has carried us through. He's stamped his character on the team's performances."'

These were generous words indeed, and there were more, as the players reckoned my presence on the pitch gave an extra momentum that enabled us to pull the game out of the fire. Eamon O'Keefe was especially generous when he said, 'Larry's professional approach to many important situations was the driving force behind our promotion. I had no doubts in my mind when I left Goodison Park for Springfield Park that we were going up. Larry made that quite clear, and has backed up his statement by encouragement, hard work and character.'

But I need to balance these great critics by saying that I had the best bunch of lads in that football league – which was why it was heartbreaking to have to split up the squad after we earned promotion. However, sadly, the economics of the game back then dictated as much. I had to make some of the toughest decisions I've ever had to make. They said that I had been a tower of strength, but, if this was true, it was also true that there had been many trying moments.

It was an exciting but also exhausting season, and then once we had been promoted there was much heartbreak. The bottom line was that I had to raise money to buy players who would help us have a shot at the Third Division title. So I pruned my professional players of twenty-one by four, and put another four on the transfer list. I let John Brown, Steve McAdam, Jeff Wright and Neil Davids go for free. Clive Evans, Jimmy Western, Mark Wignal, Mick Quinn and Brian Taylor (who was on loan from Preston) had to go as well. I simply had to prune and transfer to raise money to buy men who could help take us to the top of the league. Popular, I was not. Not everyone was unhappy, though; Alex Cribley, Peter Houghton and Colin Methven were offered new improved contracts. When 26-year-old Neil Davids spoke to the *Sunday Times*, he generously told them, 'Nobody is going to pick me up as there are a lot of better players on the heap than me, but playing with Larry Lloyd was something; it was really smashing.'

I tell you, that pruning was the toughest part of management. Having to call a lad in and say, 'Sorry, son, you don't fit into my plans,' was horrible. Neil Davids was a great pal, and giving him the chop was particularly gutting. My decision made him one of 500 professional footballers out of work in England.

But, on a more positive note, it was our 3–1 victory over Mansfield that ensured our promotion. I was very emotional. In a sense, it felt like a greater personal achievement than winning my four England caps and European medals. I was only one of eleven men back then, but this time it was all down to me. I had created a team and then played in it, and that was hugely satisfying, and probably my finest hour. To have gained promotion in my first full season was beyond my wildest dreams.

As the champagne corks popped, the people of Wigan forgot all about those music-hall jokes about their dilapidated pier.

But it wasn't too long before the champers ran out, as, the following season, everything went pear shaped and, after losing eight matches in a row, I was axed as the manager in April 1983.

It was all very depressing, and chairman Freddie Pye was feeling down about sacking me; he said he didn't like having to tell me to go, but sack me he did. Bobby Charlton took over as a temporary manager; perhaps he thought he'd discovered the secret of management, but it seemed that Bobby didn't really want it on a permanent basis. Had I failed the Division Three test?

It was clear we weren't going up, but, that said, we weren't in danger of going down either. All in all, I was proud of what I'd achieved at Wigan, and I had enjoyed the whole experience enormously. Wigan is a place of character, and the characters who live there are smashing.

The club being promoted had been an uplifting experience for the club, the players and the fans. It brought great joy to a team that worked hard and deserved some success.

I had discovered some talent too! There were three lads in particular – Steve Walsh, David Lowe and John Butler – who did really well and went on to play for bigger clubs. So yes, considering everything, managing Wigan had been a positive chapter in the life and times of Larry Lloyd.

Wigan were happy to keep me on as a player, but I was coming to the conclusion I'd had enough. In the end, it was the combination of my failing mind *and* body that led to my retiring from professional football.

It was the winter of 1982 and my back was beginning to play up again. I went to see my original surgeon, the brilliant Bill Whatmore. Bill told me that I needed another operation, but, if I went on playing football and was to need a third operation, it was likely I would end up in a wheelchair.

I decided to have one more game, and it just so happened that, of all teams, we were up against Mansfield.

Most matches had been postponed that week due to horrendous weather conditions and frozen pitches, but the referee decided that Field Mill wasn't too bad and we should play.

The incident which confirmed my decision to retire happened about 30 minutes into the game. We were already 1–0 down when the ball was lofted into our box. I was marking this big young centre-forward who, along with me, challenged for the ball.

I totally mistimed my leap and ended up heading the back of his head. Ten years earlier, it would have been him hitting the deck like a pack of cards, with his head spinning like a cartoon character, seeing stars. But this time it was me lying prostrate on the freezing ground, wondering what the fuck was happening.

It gets worse. Imagine the scene. I landed in a puddle of icy slush with blood pouring down my cheek. It was one degree above freezing and we were losing the match with only one man and his proverbial dog as spectators. Then, on to the pitch ran our trainer, Kenny Banks, who proceeded to squeeze an ice-cold sponge on to the back of my neck.

It was sitting there in the middle of that dark cold pitch with blood running down my cheek and freezing water running down my back that I knew it was game over. Not for me a swansong of a tremendous goal. Oh, no! Still, shit happens, and we don't all get happy endings.

I was going back to Nottingham, not to the Forest to be a Merry Man, but to rivals Notts County. Desperate measures, I suppose, but you have to put food on the table and buy a pint now and again.

But it would have run smoother if it wasn't for a certain young man called Justin Fashanu.

CHAPTER 21

NOTTS COUNTY

WIGAN HAD SACKED me but wanted to keep me on as a player, but out of the blue I received a request from Notts County chairman Jack Dunnett (former Labour MP in Nottingham) to meet him at his house. After just ten minutes, he offered me a job as team manager under Jimmy Sirrel – *the* one and only Jimmy Sirrel, who was an absolute legend at Notts County.

I made a grave error at this club by listening far too much to what Jimmy had to say, instead of trusting my own judgement and doing my own thing, as I had at Wigan. I made an assumption that this great expert knew best.

Les Bradd was a former Notts County player who had done a great job for me at Wigan, but, now retired, had taken a job in his old club's commercial department. He told me later that, in his opinion, I had gone soft when I went to Notts County. I think he had a point.

All the time I was there, I felt unwelcome, and this did my

confidence levels no good whatsoever. I think this had much to do with my Forest connections. I had the feeling, which was later to be proved right, that people wanted me to fail. I eventually did.

There's one incident I'll never forget. It was so humiliating. An annual general meeting had been called where I came face to face with shareholders and fans. Chairman Jack Dunnett was present, as was Jimmy Sirrel, company secretary Neil Hook and yours truly.

Jimmy was on his feet, answering questions from the floor, when a question was put to him. 'Jimmy? Why the hell are we near the bottom of the table again?'

Jimmy pointed a bony finger at me and replied to the shareholder, 'Ask him!' Then he sat down and threw me to the wolves.

I could have passed the question on to the chairman, but, to be honest, I was deflated, and couldn't be arsed, so simply took the abuse. The buck stopped with me.

It was a strange period for me. We were relegated during my first season, yet the chairman put me in full charge of football affairs. Then he told me, 'Raise one million pounds in six weeks or I fold the club.'

Consequently, I had to sell three of my best players, which, as you can imagine, I was not happy about.

With no money to bring new players in, as the money from the sales only paid off debts, I was left with players I thought were unprofessional. Many were heavy drinkers and some were even on drugs. On top of this, I inherited one of the strangest players I've ever met in my life – Justin Fashanu.

He was already there when I was appointed and he surrounded himself with religious people. One day, I picked up the morning paper and one of the sports headlines read, 'I'm going to score 25 goals for God.'

I sat there scratching my head. It was February, and by this point of the season he had only managed to score two goals. So I buzzed the dressing room, and asked Fash to come and see me.

I looked him straight in the eye. 'Fash, you say you're going to score 25 goals for God, but what about for me? I tell you, *Him* upstairs is quite capable of looking after Himself, whereas I, on the other hand, am under terrible pressure down here.'

Quite bizarrely, he never uttered a word. He simply turned and walked away.

A few weeks later, when we were struggling so badly that my job was on the line, I went for a meal in town with John Robertson. Sitting there, minding our own business, we were interrupted by Fash, who, it would appear, had something profound to tell us. 'Larry,' he began. (He didn't address me as *Boss*, which put my back up straight away.) 'Remember, it took the Israelites 2,000 years to come out of the wilderness.'

I shot an incredulous look at Robbo. We'd had a drink or two by then, and my patience was nil. 'Fash, I ain't got 2,000 fucking minutes to save my job. Now fuck off.'

Poor old Fash. I guessed he wasn't terribly well, and not long after Cloughie confirmed he'd been a complete nightmare when he had played under him at Notts Forest. 'I made a terrible mistake,' said Clough. 'I was a fool to spend one million pounds on a guy who had made his name on *Match of the Day* for scoring "The Goal of the Season" against Liverpool. He was *so* frustrating and infuriating – not at all the star he was supposed to be.'

Well, I had already found that little gem out for myself! The guy was not well. On the pitch, he was maddening by missing easy chances. According to Cloughie, Fash walked into his office one day and declared, 'I've found God!'

Quick as a flash, he came back at Fash, 'Oh! Good, you can get him to sign your cheques.'

It would appear Cloughie had it harder than me. 'On the pitch he used to throw his boots into the crowd, and off the pitch he would park his Jeep wherever he damn well pleased. But it was probably his frequenting a notorious gay club that got to me the most. I am pretty ashamed to say now that I shouldn't have been so intolerant with him. But that's how I am.'

I had the same sort of trouble with him, and I too had no patience.

I can't say he wasn't pleasant, and at times he was likeable, but he was a liar and a wind-up. I wanted to get rid of him, but I wouldn't have gone to the extremes Cloughie went to by calling the police and getting him removed. 'Please arrest my centre-forward,' he reportedly pleaded, and two officers came and escorted him away. Seems extreme – that's Cloughie!

I became convinced Fash was suffering from dreadful levels of paranoia and delusion, and when he committed suicide I can't say I was surprised. He'd been living in the States, and had been accused of molesting a 17-year-old boy, charges he denied in his suicide note. It was all very sad.

On a cheerier note, I have a little story from my time at Notts County when we went on tour to Kenya to play Mombasa and Nairobi. We were also going to be spending a few days relaxing. There was one word of warning. Apparently, sexual diseases were rife in that part of the world, and so we were told to be very careful.

Travelling out on the plane, I sat and had a chat with the club's doctor. 'What about these sexually transmitted diseases?' I asked. 'Just how bad are they?'

'Bad. Very bad. But there's not too much to worry about because

I've got 50 shots of penicillin with me, and there are only 15 of you. So, if the worst comes to the worst, we've plenty of medication.'

On the way home, we had another chat. 'Did you have to use any of those injections Doc?'

'A few.' He was being non-committal.

'How many you got left then?'

'Three.'

Talk about taking risks! I asked him who he'd given shots to, but ethically he was bound by confidentiality. I couldn't help but smile. Dirty bastards!

Another memory I have concerns an ageing Jimmy Sirrel, who had become wizened old 'Mr Notts County'. We were due to play a home game and, as usual, I arrived at the ground around midday. I noticed Jimmy was already there, which was unusual.

Pushing open the door to his office, and already holding a mug of coffee for myself, I asked if he'd like a cup.

'Thanks, Larry, I will, and can you put a shot in it?'

He seemed a bit distant, kind of tired. 'Are you OK, Jimmy?'

'Not really, Larry. My wife passed away this morning.'

'Christ, Jimmy, what are you doing here? Go home!'

'Why go home? I can't do nothing there.'

'B-but where is she?'

'She's still at home. I called the doctor and they're waiting now for the boys with the bag to come and take her.'

There were no tears, just a numb disbelief that the woman he'd spent his whole life with had gone. We sat there with our coffees (I'd had a shot too) and all I can remember was in my head I kept saying, *Oh, dear, oh, dear.*

All in all, my time at Notts County was a challenging affair. As well as the hassles with the club and people working against me, the fans also turned very cruelly on me, and started not only abusing me – which I can handle – but abusing my family as well. I had a teenage daughter and I wasn't having any ignorant arsehole throwing abuse her way. It was awful, and at one stage I jumped out of the trainer's box into the crowd and chased the filthy-mouthed bastard out of the ground.

Soon afterwards, I decided it was time to quit. Enough was enough. After telling the chairman about the way I was feeling, he agreed to let me go. He paid the rest of my contract in full and even gave me a car.

I know he liked me and maybe he was letting me know that I had been given a rough ride by the club who used to be rivals to the Nottingham Forest that I love. Perhaps that had been the root of all the bad feeling.

But life has its ups and downs; as the songs says, 'Life is a roller coaster'.

Now I was to venture into the fantastic world of commentating and PR, a job I loved most of the time. But, when tragedy strikes and you have to deliver horrific news, the words stick in your throat.

CHAPTER 22

BACHELOR DAYS

MY LATE THIRTIES were great years — I call them my bachelor days. I had kind of got my head around women, and were taking them for what they were — aliens from another planet. I was still tall, darkish with a few grey highlights and handsome, with the sideburns trimmed down a bit to keep up with the fashion.

I'd often thought I'd like to run a pub, so, when I took on the first of three pubs I was to run in Nottingham, it felt right. I enjoyed this type of work, and the mix of working in PR at Nottingham Forest and doing my radio show was perfect. Life was sweet.

I was thoroughly enjoying the commentary work with Central Radio in Nottingham; being a pundit suited my personality.

The first pub I leased was right opposite the Royal Theatre in the heart of the city, aptly called The Stage Door. Dennis Waterman and Rula Lenska came to the opening and this heralded a time when my troubles felt far away. The pub did very well — the location was good and the atmosphere inside was brilliant.

Initially, I ran the pub on my own, but as the place became really popular I took on a manager to free me up to enjoy myself a little – or a lot. Don't forget, training and playing football at the highest level had meant one hell of a lot of hard work and not much else. Attempting to get your body in tip-top shape and keep it there takes one hell of a lot of discipline. Keeping your place in the first team becomes an obsession.

Now I had time to enjoy golf with mates and widen my horizons. Don't get me wrong, I was still Lloydie the footballer, and kept my finger on the pulse of everything that was going on in the leagues. There wasn't much I didn't know about. I knew (still do) who was where in the league, who was managing whom and which players were playing at the top of their game.

I could afford to drive smart cars by now. First I had a BMW, but, as my dream car had always been a Mercedes, it was inevitable that one day – even if it was only for a spell – I would drive a Merc.

I had made enough money to buy a big house, and the fact that Yolanda and Damian were both living with me by then made everything fantastic. My kids being with their Pop was really the cherry on top of a well-iced cake for the three of us.

I wasn't at home an awful lot, but they were well into their teens by then and were forging lives and friendships of their own.

I had a couple of steady girlfriends (not at the same time I hasten to add; I was too conservative for any of that malarkey!) who enjoyed staying at home with Yolanda and Damian when I was working. They all got along well – if they hadn't, the girl would have been history. My kids came first. And when they started dating themselves I was very overprotective.

I have to tell you how awful it was to see some grubby lad holding my princess Yolanda's perfect hand! It's not easy for us dads to watch young hormonal teenagers lusting after our daughters. Time flashes by so quickly that it seems as if it was only yesterday you too were trying your luck, so you know exactly what is going through their mucky minds.

I feel a little ashamed to say the first poor lad that accompanied Yolanda home came in for a lot of stick. I demanded respect, and insisted he addressed me as Mr Lloyd. He strolled through the door and cheerily chirped, 'Hi, Larry.'

I grabbed him by the throat and growled, 'That's Mr Lloyd to you.'

How rotten of me was that! Was I intimidating him or teasing the poor lad? Well, I meant to tease but have a sneaky feeling Yolanda's first love felt intimidated.

The truth of it was I wanted him to clear off and take his rampant hormones with him. I remember explaining to the terrified lad that if he ever hurt my princess I would break his legs. But when I broke out into a wide grin he got the message I was all hot air and liked him really. That was when he decided he'd hang around a while longer.

Damian and I got along well together. Home was a safe and happy place, and they both had plenty of freedom while I was at work. Damian was more of an introvert and enjoyed his own company, although, of course, he did have some close friends who came and went.

Yolanda had a great circle of friends. She was an outgoing girl who enjoyed fashion and all the other girlie things associated with adolescence. Two of her best friends, Claire and Amanda, were always at our house and Yolanda told me just recently that they all still talk about those 'good old days'. I miss them too. They were good times for all of us.

Weekends began on a Thursday and didn't stop until Sunday night.

One of the best Nottingham clubs was The Maddison, which was opposite The Stage Door – very handy indeed. After shutting up the pub, I would enjoy a fabulous night clubbing, and it would go on to the small hours of the morning until I was starving hungry and went for a steak breakfast in an all-night café.

There were two other clubs I used to frequent. One was owned by a good golfing pal of mine. We nicknamed it Jurassic Park because of the old dinosaurs that went there on the pull.

The Black Orchid was another favourite, and had the reputation of being one of the most popular clubs in the area.

As I said, I had three pubs in all during my bachelor days in Nottingham. The second two were not as popular as The Stage Door. The Bendigo was far too quiet and I didn't keep it for long. The third was The Trent Hotel.

I truly enjoyed those bachelor days when I answered to no one and lived under the same roof as my lovely kids – with me taking care of them and them of me.

When Robbo's marriage hit the rocks, his wife Sally thought I was to blame. I find it quite astonishing and slightly amusing that the aggrieved partner always blames their other half's best friend for the demise of their relationship. It reminds me of the classic comedy *The Likely Lads*, aired during the sixties and seventies, when wife Thelma gets so wound up about her husband Bob being, in her mind, led astray by tricky Terry. But I had nothing to do with their break-up – that was between them.

Sally and Robbo had had a good marriage, but it had been tested severely when they lost their darling daughter Jessica, who tragically died when she was just 13 years old. Life can be such a bastard.

Damian once said to me, 'You and Robbo would do anything for each other, wouldn't you, Dad?' He was right. He's still right.

When Robbo became a bachelor too, he would spend lots of time at our house. He'd go to the fridge, open the door and ask in his Scottish accent, 'What's for eatin'?', then proceed to devour all the delicious food inside.

He was a bit strapped for cash at the time (he won't mind me saying that because later when I was strapped he came to my rescue).

He was working as a scout for Martin O'Neill, who was managing Wycombe Wanderers, and the poor bastard often found himself unable to find the petrol money to get himself there. Of course, I helped him out – that's what mates do. I can't stress enough how much he has done for me over the years when I have been broke, and still, today, when I come over to Nottingham from my home in Spain, he is happy for me to stay at his.

If I was innocent of being instrumental in the breakdown of his first marriage, I am proud to say I *was* able to help out when he met – in his own words – 'the most beautiful woman called Sharyl'. He came rushing into the pub asking for a 'sub', so he could take her out on a date. That makes me a hero, doesn't it?

Sharyl became his second wife and they have two fabulous boys now, Andrew and Mark.

If Robbo was my best mate, Martin O'Neill wasn't too far behind. I got to know him pretty well over the years, and I like him a lot. He's quite some character. He studied law in Ireland, but didn't complete his degree as the pull to play football was greater. But there was nothing he couldn't tell you about serial killers. He used to spend hours in the galleries in the Old Bailey listening to grisly cases of murder. Having been present at the trials of the Yorkshire Ripper and the Black Panther, he amassed a tremendous knowledge about such monsters.

Martin is a very, very clever man, and I am not surprised in the least that he has stayed at the top of his profession. Being awarded the OBE for his services in sport was right and just.

Now tell me something, why is that, just as everything is going well, shit happens? Life was so sweet, and I didn't for one moment visualise it would ever change. But change it did – and it all happened in a relatively short space of time.

I figured I would get rid of two of my pubs and concentrate on The Stage Door. After all, I also had my radio work and PR job at Nottingham Forest to keep me busy.

Then the brewery saw how well this city-centre pub was doing. Of course it bloody well was – I'd built up the trade so much that the place was heaving. But they decided they wanted it back to turn it into a 'managed' pub. To force me out, they increased my rent to a point where both they, and I, knew the business couldn't stand it. They won and I left.

It was a bastard; I had enjoyed the pub business.

But there was worse to come and, although the Bible says you should forgive, I will never forgive the man who I consider ran me out of Nottingham Forest and my dream jobs.

CHAPTER 23

WHEN PLATT CAME TO NOTTINGHAM

I felt so sorry for the Nottingham Forest fans when David Platt was given the management job at Forest. They wanted Martin O'Neill or Roy Evans. I was working at Century radio then and I spoke to the fans all the time. Being involved with PR at the club, I was as incensed as they were when Platt began making what were, in our opinions, dreadful mistakes by spending fortunes on players that did bugger all to pull the club out of the trouble they were in — he was supposed to help, not hinder.

AFTER MORE THAN 30 years of living and breathing the world of football, I ran into the most unpleasant man I have ever had the misfortune to meet. I won't say I know him, because I don't think many people really know him. I know for a fact I'm not the only person, fan or otherwise, that feels this way. His name is David Platt, and our paths crossed — I mean really crossed — at Nottingham Forest when he was appointed manager.

Radio commentary had taught me so much more about the whole world of football. I had played the game, now I was analysing and questioning every angle of it. Communicating closely with the fans was a joy as well as a big learning curve. I enjoyed the light-hearted banter, and got stuck into any controversy with the same passion I'd applied to defending my teams.

I snapped up the PR job I was offered at Nottingham Forest, and thoroughly enjoyed working at something I was very good at.

In between the days of 'The Master Manager' (a nickname Clough was deservedly given) and the arrival of David Platt at Nottingham Forest, there were three other managers appointed.

My mate Frank Clark took over when Clough left and his reign lasted three years. It became apparent that he was going to achieve an instant return to the Premiership. He had been fortunate enough to inherit those who hadn't been sold off or let go by Cloughie, so he had a chance of a fair shot at success and guiding the club to promotion, which is exactly what he did!

Going up was sweet for the boys, and even sweeter when they finished third in the league, qualifying for the UEFA Cup. You could say Forest had a brief spell back in the glory days (well, not quite!) in 1994/95.

A game the fans remember well is an away clash between Forest and Manchester United, played at Old Trafford, when naughty boy Stan Collymore and Stuart Pearce scored goals. I think Stan was at his very best then; he was on fire. It was a dark day for the fans when he was sold on to Liverpool in June 1995 for a then English record fee of £8.4 million, as the goals dried up, and it seemed to signal the end for Frank.

A nightmarish relegation battle was on again, and it was only to be a matter of time before Frank was sacked and Stuart Pearce was employed as a temporary player-manager.

Stuart did well by lifting the club out of the relegation zone. He inspired a brief revival in the club, and on a personal level he was voted Premiership manager of the month in January 1997. Stuart was tipped for the permanent job, but the powers that be decided to choose someone 'more experienced' and took on Crystal Palace's Dave Bassett.

Forest finished the season on the bottom rung of the league and were relegated. Bassett was sacked in January 1999, and it became a case of move over, Dave, and make room for 'Big Ron'.

Ron Atkinson was given the incentive of a £1 million bonus if he could prevent relegation. He couldn't, and Forest went down.

The fans didn't warm to poor old Ron, which wasn't surprising as he didn't exactly endear himself to anyone who loved the team.

The dozy bugger made no friends when he climbed into the wrong dugout in his first game in charge. They were playing Arsenal, and in true Ron style he managed to make a joke of it by saying he thought Dennis Bergkamp was sitting on *his* bench. Not many people laughed; in fact, there wasn't much too smile about at all at Nottingham Forest throughout this dismal period. Ron's managerial record with Forest was: Played 16, Won 4, Drew 2, Lost 10. Needless to say, a new manager of splendid calibre was needed. Was the tide about to turn for Nottingham Forest? Hmm... hardly!

The misery went on and on for everyone concerned and the arrival of the new man in charge meant personal disaster for me.

It came as a surprise to everyone when it was announced that David Platt had landed the job. There had been much speculation about who should become the next manager. You could have knocked me down with a feather when Platt got the job. I didn't know him then, I just knew *of* him, and what I'd heard and saw was pretty impressive. But everyone, including me, thought Martin

O'Neill was going to get it. There was chanting at matches of 'Martin's coming home' and 'O'Neill is a Forest fan'. Other names were suggested, including my mate John Robertson. Stuart Pearce was also a strong contender, as was Roy Evans, and even Brian Little was suggested.

But the fans wanted Martin – no doubt about it, he was their favourite choice.

The truth was revealed one morning when I was in the reception area at the City Ground and I saw Nigel Doughty hanging around. Nobody knew who he was but I recognised him from two and a half years before when he was involved in the original takeover at Forest. I therefore knew all about his investments in the club.

'Hello, Nigel.' I held my hand out to greet him and then suggested we had a coffee in the Robin Hood Suite.

'Thank Christ somebody has rescued me,' he breathed.

This just so happened to be the very same morning of the press conference with Platt.

So I said to him, 'Where did this come from, Nigel? Martin, yes, Roy Evans, yes, even perhaps Brian Little… But where in God's name has Platt come from?'

He looked in his briefcase and pulled out a file. I'm telling you, it had not been put together that morning! It contained pictures of every goal Platt had ever scored. There were also clever comments written by him in Italian papers. Oh! There it was in black and white – the dossier that had been built up over a very long time.

I looked at Nigel. 'You have been targeting this guy for quite a while, haven't you?'

His response was, 'Don't believe all you read in the newspapers.'

Well, I didn't need him to give me this gem of advice; I knew only too well that what they don't know they make up to get a good story.

Well, well, so it wasn't going to be Martin after all. It was a bit of a bugger when all the speculation was over. It had been good fun. Lots of red herrings had been thrown in, and I even set up a rumour that it was going to be me!

Oh, if only one of these great masters of the game had landed that job back in 1999! But they wanted a manager of experience to sort out the mess at Forest, and it would seem they believed they'd got their man in Platt.

I loved Nottingham Forest and, like everyone else, I simply wanted the best man for the job. My attitude was: 'I don't know the lad, none of us here knows him, but we've watched him play for Arsenal, England, and in Italy, so he must be pretty good.' But none of us knew him personally.

During my first meeting with him, I was impressed. He talked a good talk. We knew a firm hand was needed and he gave the impression he could deliver it. But where did 'talking' ever get anyone? Well, as it happened, it seemed it had got Platt everywhere. It was the follow-up, the all-important action and wise decision-making that went up the fucking wall.

I was happily employed in the public relations office at the time. It was a job I was thoroughly suited to, as I got on very well with both the players and the general public. One of my jobs was to go into the dressing room as the players arrived for training in the mornings and get them to sign shirts, cards and footballs that I would later distribute to the individuals and charities that requested them.

Platt's predecessors, Dave Bassett and Ron Atkinson, used to welcome me. Ron and I often used to talk about the successful days we'd enjoyed at Forest. Working there had been a pleasure and we had all rubbed along together well.

There are so many 'if onlys' in mind about this turning point in my life. If only the board had renewed Ron's contract and given him a real chance to sort the club out. If only Martin O'Neill and Robbo had taken over as a team – that would have been really brilliant. If only *anyone* but Platt had got the job, Nottingham Forest and I would have been saved. I know that sounds dramatic, but that's because it was!

Our poor fans. They had been elevated to glory under Clough, and now they were plummeted to the depths of despair.

Platt made so many bad decisions, wasting millions on useless Italian players and crippling the club with debt. It was so wrong! He paid fortunes for players who turned out to be totally non-productive. This catalogue of errors plunged Forest into a downward spiral that has proved, to this very day, impossible to come back from.

One day something really embarrassing happened and this is an example of the behaviour I came to abhor. Carol, Platt's secretary, asked me if I would get a shirt signed by all the players for Platt, as he was going to a charity function. I said it was no problem. As I was walking across the car park towards the dressing room, I noticed Platt standing by the door talking to two reporters. I nodded 'good morning' and went to pass.

With that, Platt stuck his arm out and barred my way; all the while he kept talking to the men with his arm locked across my chest. The reporters were visibly shocked at his aggressive manner, and shuffled uncomfortably before quickly making their exits.

Eventually he spoke. 'The players aren't happy about you going into the dressing room.'

I checked this with the captain, Steve Chettle. If this was really the case, I would listen to the reasons and react accordingly. After all, I wasn't an unreasonable man, and as I'd matured I'd lost a lot of my hot-headed ways. But Steve was baffled – it was the first he'd heard of this.

I was more astonished than angry, and my demeanour showed this. I challenged him. 'Listen David, this is part of my job, and the charity element is really important. Anyway, I was on my way to get a shirt signed that *you* had requested.'

He was dismissive again and just stated coldly that the players' dressing room was sacred. As if I didn't know what a dressing room was all about after a long career in the game.

I shook my head in sheer wonderment. 'Can I remind you that, as far as club levels go, I have frequented far more sacred, pressure-filled dressing rooms in my career than you can dream of, pal!'

I'd clearly hit a nerve in a man with a fragile ego that he wore alongside the chip on his shoulder. He promptly turned his back on me and slammed the door in my face.

Several weeks later, I was called in to see the new chief executive, Mark Arthur. He informed me that my services were no longer required at Nottingham Forest Football Club. I was in bits, really gutted.

I guessed Platt was behind this so I went to see him. But yet again he was dismissive in his attitude: 'Nothing to do with me.' Not much! Wanker!

My other job was sports broadcaster on the local Century radio station. As I said, I had been a co-commentator for years, covering all Forest's games, as well as some for Leicester, Derby and Notts County.

It was while I was working for this station that, one sunny afternoon in spring, I went off to Hillsborough to commentate on an FA Cup semi-final where Nottingham Forest were due to play Liverpool. It was 15 April and a day none of us shall ever forget.

217

CHAPTER 24

HILLSBOROUGH

THE DARKEST DAYS for football are when a tragedy happens and the lives of fans are lost. The effects of such devastation never go away, but live on in the hearts of the bereaved. As I was so closely involved with Liverpool FC, the Hillsborough disaster hit me hard.

Hillsborough had been the venue of many an FA Cup match, and because of a scare in 1981, when a crush had occurred at a semi-final between Spurs and Wolverhampton Wanderers (there were 38 injuries but no fatalities) in the same Leppings Lane stand, Sheffield Wednesday decided to alter the design. They divided the area into three separate pens, believing this would be safer.

When Sheffield Wednesday were promoted to Division One in 1985 (the year of the Heysel tragedy), they made more improvements by further dividing it into five sections. As it so happened, Liverpool and Nottingham Forest had played against each other the previous year, but without any incident.

Not so in 1989.

It was a warm Saturday afternoon and I was at Hillsborough to commentate on the semi-final of the FA Cup. We were all looking forward to a great match but it all went horribly wrong. Even as I write, the memory fills me with horror.

It was dreadfully stuffy in that commentary box, but that didn't matter; I was about to enjoy a match between two teams that were close to my heart – Liverpool and Nottingham Forest.

I knew these fans intimately, just as they knew me.

The match, like all FA Cup matches, was due to kick off at 3 o'clock, but it was a little before this when I realised something wasn't right.

Don't forget, I was commentating and therefore my focus was on the pitch and not the crowd. I remember thinking there was a lot of movement at the top of the Leppings Lane stand, but I certainly didn't have a clue about the hell unfolding at the bottom where young people were already fighting for their lives.

It was a few minutes into the game when it was clear that the Liverpool fans who had been allocated tickets at the Leppings Lane End were in serious trouble. I could see a crowd of fans piling on to the pitch. It was total chaos.

But it soon became clear that something awful was occurring, and those Liverpool fans were the victims of a terrible tragedy. They were suffocating, dying in front of me, in front of the nation.

Peter Beardsley had just hit the crossbar with a fierce shot, but my eyes were drawn back to the Leppings Lane End. I was transfixed. It was unbelievable. Then the referee called a halt to the game and the players were rushed off to their dressing rooms.

I saw people clutching hoardings, and advertising boards were being broken up and used as stretchers. It was pure chaos.

Then I watched a spectacle happening directly below that chilled me to the core. This copper had run into my view, and in his arms he was carrying the limp body of a young girl. He laid her on the pitch and began to give her mouth-to-mouth resuscitation. The poor bastard was showing signs of desperation and after some time he sat back and shook his head. Tears were streaming down his face as he knew he had lost the fight. She was dead.

The next moments are a blur to me. In one sense, it all unfolded so quickly, but time also seemed to be moving in slow motion.

Des Lynam, who was commentating for TV, was telling the nation, the thousands of people watching the match from pubs or in their homes, 'There has been a tragedy at Hillsborough and there are many dead.' They were seeing more than we were – but we were bang in the middle of a nightmare.

It would become apparent to me a little later that the tragedy began to unfold outside the stadium about half an hour before kick-off, when most of the Nottingham Forest fans were already in another area of the ground.

Some of the Liverpool supporters had arrived late from their journey across the Pennines, and, for various reasons, a crowd of approximately 2,000 were building up against the turnstiles. They were becoming anxious as the minutes to kick-off were ticking away, and the police must have sensed this. By 2.45, the numbers had swelled to more than 5,000.

Some fans managed to squeeze through, and these arrived inside the ground out of breath and sweating profusely.

Then a police officer apparently slid open the steel concertina door of gate C and everything spun out of control, as fans spilled into pens that were already uncomfortably full. I heard that many died standing up, and those at the front were crushed. This was the crush that I was observing.

The scale of this nightmare soon became clear. I watched with a sickness rising in my stomach as the lifeless bodies of children and teenagers were laid out on the pitch. There was pandemonium for a time, as people screamed out for loved ones, and police and ambulance staff fought to save lives. Lost souls were stumbling in groups of two, trying in vain to comfort each other, their pale faces twisted in anguish.

Then frenzied activity gave way to an eerie silence. Gone were the wailing sirens and gone were the lives of 96 people.

I stood in the commentary box at 4.50 – the scheduled end of the game – and, apart from abandoned clothes and littered programmes, the ground was empty. The bodies had been taken to the stadium's gymnasium, laid out, and covered, waiting for some poor sod to have to come and identify their father, brother, sister or, worse, child. It was pure hell.

Finally, I made my way to my car. En route, I passed a solitary Liverpool supporter sitting on the kerb with his head in his hands, sobbing. He was still wearing his red and white scarf. I drove home in silence, while trying in vain to absorb what I had just witnessed. I thought about the game of football, and life in general. I remember thinking it was just another fucking football match! How could young lives be taken like that? What a horrific way to die. I couldn't sleep that night. My head was filled with the images of the day.

In the morning, of course, the television and newspapers were filled with pictures and stories of the Hillsborough tragedy. There was a photograph of the copper I had seen trying to revive the young girl. It was surreal.

Horror stories began to emerge, as the dead were named one by one. I wondered about some lads I'd had a pint with in a pub before the match. Had they, I wondered, ever made it back home to

Liverpool? God, it makes you think. It was a black day for Liverpool. It was a black day for football.

I heard some years later that Steven Gerrard, one of our greatest Liverpool players of all time, had lost his cousin at Hillsborough. Like Steven (who was nine at the time of the tragedy), his cousin Jon Paul (the same age) had been Liverpool crazy. What a crushing sense of loss.

One has to feel for Kenny Dalglish. He was playing for Liverpool on the night of the Heysel tragedy and was manager of Liverpool at the Hillsborough tragedy. But these weren't the first harrowing matches he'd been present at.

In 1971, he attended the Old Firm derby at Ibrox where 66 people died as stairway 13 of the ageing stadium collapsed, while fans left the ground shortly before the end of the match. Kenny's had a wonderful career, but he's also had more than his fair share of experiencing first-hand the danger involved for loyal fans.

If anything at all can be said in an attempt to ease the pain of such loss, what we can say is that crowd safety improved enormously in the wake of that fateful afternoon. The laws were changed and all-seater stadiums were ordered. The face of football was changed forever.

I went home and hugged my children close – as I'm certain so many more parents did too.

CHAPTER 25

WHAT HAPPENED TO NOTTINGHAM FOREST NEXT

I PRESENTED AN hour-long football phone-in programme six days a week, which, after a while, began to pull in a vast amount of listeners. The figures had soared by 60 per cent during the second half of the 1999/2000 season, and the listener participation was excellent, so I knew I was doing a good job.

Forest, on the other hand, were not playing well at all. All was not as it should have been in the camp, and the first half of the season saw very poor results. Yet Platt was spending fortunes of the club's money –upwards of £12 million on new players. Naturally, my radio show was inundated with pissed-off Forest supporters who were seriously critical of the manager.

Football fans are never slow to verbalise any complaints where their beloved team are concerned! And, to be honest, I had to agree with much of their criticism.

I wasn't the only one to speak out against what Platt was doing to Nottingham Forest, as Cloughie also had harsh words to say. 'When I took part in a local radio discussion, I gave Platt some stick on air,' he said. 'I couldn't help it, because I meant it, and, if ever he makes contact with me, I'll give him some more. As far as I'm concerned, he left my old club in a terrible state.'

Hear, hear, Cloughie! My sentiments exactly! Poor old Cloughie has passed away now, but I'm still standing, and am proud to speak up for the both of us.

I read a little piece on the Internet about my last days commentating for the local radio station in Nottingham that said I was barely able to mention Platt's name without accompanying it with a sneer. How damn right was that writer? Bloody right his name was always accompanied by what I'd actually call a growl.

That summer, after working hard for Forest and putting lots of energy into my radio jobs, I went off to Cyprus for a well-deserved holiday, happy in the knowledge I'd done a good job for the radio station by increasing their figures.

I needed to wind down after travelling the country commentating on matches and hosting my show. But little did I know that, as I was sunning myself, dark forces were moving against me.

When I returned, I discovered that a larger radio company had taken over the local radio station. I didn't anticipate this would present me with any problems as they were very sports orientated. When I was called to a meeting with the new bosses, I went armed with my unbelievable listening statistics, hoping I might even get a rise.

But, before I could even say good morning (let alone show any stats), a fellow I'd never met before (and who had never even listened to any of my shows) told me my services were no longer required. He told me his instructions had come from London, and that I was to leave the premises immediately. I felt like a fucking criminal!

I investigated what had preceded my being sacked, and really shouldn't have been surprised by what was uncovered.

All I know is that local radio stations have a commitment to cover every game Nottingham Forest played, and therefore rely on the co-operation of the club – everyone from players to management. They had no alternative but to ask me to leave. It was unbelievable in a sporting profession.

I can't express to you enough how upset I was. I was totally devastated – gutted. What added insult to injury was that, while I had been in Cyprus, my old mate Garry Birtles (who, incidentally, confessed to me once how much he hated football and would rather be carpet fitting!) was interviewed for the job.

OK, all's fair in love and war, but in my book you don't stab a mate in the back, but, if you are going to, then come clean and talk about it. But nope, not a word of explanation or apology came my way. The least he could have done was forewarn me that I was in for the chop.

That whole period was horrendous for me, both personally and professionally. Betrayal is a rotten feeling. Not knowing who you can trust is confusing and losing a decent income as well as a much-loved job is a terrible blow. I literally fell apart at this time. It was all so unnecessary, and when I look back this was the beginning of my falling into a terrible pit of despair.

David Platt has much to answer for, and I am not talking personally now, but about a club that means so much to me.

Having wasted millions of pounds, he finally turned to the Academy and looked to the youth to get him out of trouble – but it was a tall order. He should be eternally grateful to Academy Director Paul Hart, who in my opinion kept him in a job that he was not worthy of for far too long.

The charming Mr Platt seems to know just who to hang around with. When he was playing football in Italy, he made good friends with Sven-Goran Eriksson who was also working with an Italian club. Fair enough, everyone is free to make friends with whomever they wish. Call me an old sceptic, but I'm one who seems to be spot on in sniffing out when someone has an ulterior motive. And what did Platt end up doing for a while? Managing the England Under 21s.

No one can take away from him that he adapted quickly to top-class football. He was given his first England cap by Bobby Robson in a friendly against Italy in 1989, and had a successful spell with Arsenal. But from here on in it would appear to me that it all went a bit wonky for him, and he was in danger of sinking.

After retiring as a player, he turned to management and travelled to Sampdoria, who were relegated under Platt's management. Allegedly, due to his lack of coaching qualifications, he was not permitted to stay, so he came back – to Nottingham Forest.

Damn and blast. Did I bear the brunt of his frustrations? I think so. That said, I wasn't the only one who he upset. His tenure at Forest was marred by several disagreements with experienced, long-serving players, leading them to be isolated from the first-team picture and subsequently released by the club.

I left the world of football with a heavy heart and moved on; I had no choice. It was all over for me.

When Paul Hart, the good guy who was patient with Platt, was appointed manager in 2001, he had one hell of a job on his hands. Terrible mistakes had been made but there was worse to come.

ITV Digital, the world's first digital terrestrial television network, which had been launched in 1998, had been losing money from the start and their collapse almost bankrupted Forest.

Given all this, Paul did pretty well in his first season with his team that was made up of youngsters. But, in 2002, the only thing that saved them from liquidation was selling off talent such as Jermaine Jenas. A string of managers since, including Joe Kinnear and Gary Megson, have presided over Forest's slide down the divisions to League One. The old Third Division!

Today Colin Calderwood is managing Nottingham Forest. He became the 12th manager in 13 years in May 2006. All we can pray is that the club keeps on plugging away and soon there will be more glory days. At the time of this book going to print, they are challenging for promotion at the top of League One.

As for me, every time I walk past the cabinet at City Ground, I gaze in at the reproduction trophies of the European Cups and a smile creeps over my face as I remember with fondness the glory days.

I wonder if the club will ever see such wonderful times again. I bloody well hope so!

CHAPTER 26

MARRIAGE, SECOND TIME AROUND

I REALLY DON'T know why one chooses to get married a second time; you might just as well buy a house for someone you don't particularly like. I've come to realise that some women have hidden agendas, and it's not always a matter of what they want as what they need.

In 1995, Yolanda was chosen to be chief bridesmaid at her best friend Jackie's wedding. Jackie had been like a second daughter to me – a really lovely young girl. It was a beautiful wedding and a great reception. I went along with Damian, and we found ourselves sitting on a table with a very pretty woman named Debbie and her family.

It would be fair to say that Damian and I were well on our way, after having spent the previous two hours at the local before setting out to the wedding, so, when I saw a young dark-haired girl, I thought, 'Why not ask her to dance?' Sadly, I don't remember much about the rest of the evening.

Three weeks later, she walked into my pub and we got chatting.

She said she had just been passing, but I think she fancied me and couldn't wait to see me again! Well, hey, I was still that tall, dark handsome man – only in my forties.

Debbie and I got on reasonably well considering the 17-year age gap, and both Yolanda and Damian liked their Pop's new girlfriend. Deb's mum and dad were totally against me, though, as they thought I was too old for their 29-year-old daughter. They wound me up so much that I took to driving up outside her house to pick her up with a brown paper bag over my face. It was all a bit of fun to lighten the tension of the parental disapproval.

I was living in my lovely house in Nottingham at the time and doing very well for myself. It was during this period that I ran three pubs which were all doing well and all in the garden was pretty rosy; even Deb's parents mellowed, and the tension eased between us. Debbie had never married before and had no children. It just seemed inevitable that we would marry.

The wedding ceremony took place in Cyprus, and Debbie looked divine in a Greek-style fitted dress (not a meringue in sight, thank God). The year was 1997, and about 20 family members and friends flew out, including my old mate Robbo. There were canapés and champagne and all was well… for a few hours.

I should have read the writing that was clearly on the wall on that lovely wedding day, but love is blind – or was for a while!

We were all in need of a siesta, so an arrangement was made whereupon we would all meet up in the evening at one of the local restaurants around nine o'clock.

I woke around eight-thirty and, after some considerable time trying, with no success, to wake my bride, I jumped in the shower and then grabbed a taxi to the restaurant that was five miles away. Our guests were already there, and the evening was a great success

– until one in the morning when a taxi screamed up, hailing the arrival of a now wide-awake Debbie. Her face was like thunder, and she didn't take kindly to the chants about missing her own wedding reception. But I'd had a great time – there was no way I was going to miss out on an evening I'd already paid for.

Some time later, Debbie decided she wanted to go to college to do a teacher-training course, which was fine, except I was supporting both of us and she didn't really use this skill. She had a temp job here and there, but nothing to speak of and certainly no dosh coming in.

Debbie seemed unsettled. Before we'd met, she spent six years living in Australia and she couldn't seem to get it out of her blood. She was forever stressing about how to earn the necessary points to get a visa to move there. She should have become a hairdresser because you get lots of points for that particular vocation. Then she had the bright idea that she would enrol in a college in Australia. My wife wanted to be a student in Australia now. Needless to say, the relationship between us began to wane. I agreed to finance her new harebrained scheme – and off she went.

My mates thought I was nuts paying for my wife to go across the other side of the world and start a new life without me, and kept asking me if I was mad. 'No' was my reply. 'I'll be glad to be fucking rid of her.' In all honesty, a man can only take so much of his wife's whinges about wanting to be elsewhere.

My take on the matter was that she'd left me to make a new life for herself. Her love affair was with Australia, not me. She had made this very clear and so by the time she left I was fine with her plans, and certainly not heartbroken.

I was confused all over again though. Oh my God! A new-age woman was beginning to get to me, and I was at a loss to know what to do. Don't forget, I'd met Sue in school during the fifties, and she had been my one and only woman until I was way into my thirties.

Debbie was born in the sixties when I was already in a relationship with my first wife and having children was just around the corner. When she was a toddler, I was playing football for my country. Her parents had been right – the age gap was just too much. For my part, I couldn't help wonder whether Debbie, like so many women of today, had some hidden agenda for marrying an older man who was financially comfortable. (Note: I said *was* financially comfortable.)

I bet there's not a man reading this that wouldn't agree with my next example of what women do, and not a woman who hasn't done it. That is: buy a dress and hide it in the wardrobe only to pull it out a few days later, put it on and, when challenged, declare, 'Oh, I've had it ages.' *Not new? My arse!*

So, instead of battling away in my head as to how to understand my wife, I got on with my life. But it was a life that had become terribly stressful. Life is often described as a rollercoaster ride, and, if that is the case, I was now being plunged into a dark tunnel. When things are going well, we imagine they will go on forever. What stupid naivety this is!

Not too long before, I had it all. Now I'd lost so much and if I was to survive I would need to sacrifice even more.

I was on a real downer and convinced I was suffering from the depressive illness called Seasonal Affective Disorder, commonly known as SAD. I thought that perhaps I should move to Spain where my body could feast on sunshine that would cheer me up.

I began to make enquiries, and the more I looked into the idea the more it appealed to me. I searched the Internet, where I found there were more than enough bars for sale. I trawled through the sites and eventually found one I fancied on the Costa del Sol. It looked perfect for me.

I hadn't been to that neck of the woods for years. I remembered loving the Marbella area though. It looked like paradise. But then I guess any place where the sun shines, the sea sparkles and the daylight goes on forever is good enough for me.

The bar I'd found was in the popular seaside resort of Fuengirola, which is situated midway between Malaga and Marbella. Why Fuengirola? I can't answer this question. All I know is that I was desperate to get away and something about that little bar appealed to me.

My first wonderful marriage was over – as was my football career. It seemed to me that everything that I had ever loved was in the past, and that hurt. Sue was in Australia, and so was Debbie. While it was true my kids were still living with me in Nottingham, they were growing rapidly into young responsible adults. The time instinctively felt right for me to spread my wings and escape from a world that was closing in on me.

Then there was the case of my rapidly diminishing finances. Anxious thoughts had been ruminating in my brain for quite some time. Should I sell my coveted medals? The answer swung between no, they are my pride and joy, living proof of my achievements, and yes, I need the money.

Each medal I held in my hand brought back its own unique memory. It might seem strange to you that, although I won three medals in Europe, the one recollection that had me in tears was that first FA Cup runners-up medal I won in 1971 when we lost the epic game against Arsenal. Maybe it was because it was all so new. Perhaps it was because I was young and yet to experience the harshness of life. Whatever, I was sad. But then, as I visualised the hilarious scene of my family climbing down from the bus at Wembley and embarrassing the hell out of me, I managed to laugh out loud all over again.

Then I closed my (by now very wet) eyes and imagined I could hear the buzz of excitement as we stood in the tunnel, followed by the deafening roar from the crowd as we ran out on to the Wembley turf.

I can see Arsenal's Charlie George lying flat on his back as he celebrated his winning goal, experiencing a 'once in a lifetime' moment. They had won in extra time. Bastards!

I recalled the crushing disappointment of losing etched on Bill Shankly's face. The devastation summed up everything. I never, ever saw that man more upset. My first major defeat in a major title had been a bitter pill for me to swallow, but I also felt the amazing togetherness of a team in mourning together.

But, in the end, I knew I simply had to sell my treasures. There really was no choice if I wanted to start all over again.

Yes, it was certainly a dark day in 2001 when my medals went on sale at Christie's. I couldn't go – it would have been far too painful to watch them go under the hammer. Instead, I waited at home for them to call, all the while remembering there were Division One medals and League Cup honours, two for the Charity Shield, two more European Cup medals I'd won with Forest in our glory days, and one for being runner-up in the World Club Championships.

It was around this time that some bright spark enlightened me that I was now unemployable. Early fifties and unemployable. That came as a shock to the system, I can tell you! How could this possibly be? But it seemed to be the truth.

My whole life had been dedicated to football. The game had meant everything to me. And in a sense my whole identity had been formed around a persona. If I wasn't Larry Lloyd, the footballer, who the fuck was I?

'Didn't you used to be Larry Lloyd?' became a familiar question. Imagine that! I was recognised wherever I went, but as a character from the past – no longer 'real'.

I suppose, in a way, I knew what they meant and why they were talking about me in the past tense. But this understanding didn't help my great sense of loss. I used to answer, 'Well, actually, believe it or not, that was the name I was given at birth and, strange as it may seem, Larry Lloyd is still my name.'

In moments when I wasn't feeling so amiable, I would growl, 'Yes, I was that man. But now I'm called fat bastard.' To watch the shocked expressions on their faces was quite funny; it even cheered me up a bit. The joy was fleeting, though, and I'd go and sink a pint or two while wondering what the fucking hell was in store for me next.

I had to get out of this dark hole. I had to get far away.

I can't tell you how many times I lifted the phone to call Christie's, only to replace the receiver and sink my head into my hands and weep.

Finally, I was brave enough (or stupid enough) to speak to the auctioneers. I was about to be informed how much the man who used to be Larry Lloyd was worth in hard cash. All the time, my brain was in overdrive. What had happened to the colossus, the brick wall who had been hailed as being gifted enough to be the next Jack Charlton?

When the phone rang, I nearly jumped out of my skin. My nerves were wrecked. The man from Christie's told me in his dulcet tones that I was worth 12 grand. Twelve fucking grand!

I'm man enough to admit that I cried my heart out. It was a dreadful moment. I felt well and truly sorry for myself. I also felt terribly ashamed. The medals should have been a legacy for my kids

– my rocks – and, in turn, theirs. I asked myself, 'Is that really all I'm worth?' I don't know how many other players have found themselves in similar dire straits, how many have also been broke and had to sell up. I heard that one of the 1966 World Cup heroes had been driven to sell his medal – I sincerely hope it's not true.

Honest to God, the sense of failure and shame was overwhelming.

Nowadays I can be more forgiving of myself – after all, life is difficult. This world we live in today is a tricky one and we have to do whatever we can to survive. I needed money and had something precious to sell, so I sold. Players of my era had a tough time when our short-lived careers were over. Nowadays, the players are earning such vast sums of money that they are able to invest in long-term retirement plans. But us old boys from the old school had no such luxury.

I was lucky enough to have had a reasonable education. If not exactly the brain of Britain, I was bright enough to survive in the world outside the game. Lots of people joke about footballers having their brains in their feet and there's a lot of truth in that saying. When you focus obsessively on one area of your life, the other areas of the brain become stagnant.

So, now I had the money from the sale of my medals, I'd found the bar in Spain I fancied buying, and Yolanda and Damian were old enough for me to move to Europe. They were both doing well in their careers, and we even had a new edition to our family: Yolanda had given birth to a beautiful daughter, Georgia.

Then guess what happened? Debbie came back from Australia and wanted to try again. Fuck me, what was I to do now?

CHAPTER 27

COSTA DEL SOL

'Lloyd left Forest for Wigan Athletic in March 1981, where he was
player-manager, he then managed Notts County. Up until 2000 Larry
was a regular and outspoken pundit for local radio station Century
106 in Nottingham, covering Forest matches. He now lives in Spain.'

ANYONE READING THE above could be forgiven for assuming
Larry Lloyd was having it large in the Spanish sunshine, but
assumptions are a terrible thing. The reality of life is usually so much
harsher and, until very recently, 'harsh' could describe my life.

People back in the UK tend to think that those of us who live
abroad are on permanent holiday. But be careful what you think –
it's probably not true!

Thousands of Brits leave the grey and drizzly weather of their
homeland, fed up with rising costs and all the other problems that
are occurring in the UK; and I was one of them.

The weather was a big factor for me. As I said, I'm sure I suffer from that depressive disorder SAD. I have always thought the dark month of January should be taken out of the calendar; at the very least, it should come with a government health warning. More people top themselves in January than in any other month – did you know that?

So there I was in January, in freezing-cold Nottingham, desperate to get away and start a new life alone in the sunshine, when Debbie returned from her mini-break in Australia.

Now call me an old sceptic, but, when I told her I was moving to Spain, suddenly she wanted to give our marriage another shot. Although my gut instinct was telling me it was all wrong, after several intense 'talks', I agreed to try again. She had not been in my plans. She was supposed to be making a new life for herself across the other side of the fucking world. A life *I* had financed. But I can't stand to see a woman cry, so it was the tears that finally swayed old softie Lloydie.

I went over to the Costa del Sol to view a few bars in early March 2001, a beautiful month in Spain. I viewed quite a few properties before I finally settled on leasing the Golf bar in Fuengirola I'd originally fancied on the Internet. Strange how often that seems to happen; it's as if the original gets stuck in your brain.

The bar cost me £8,000. Money had become such a worry, but this was affordable.

In April, I renovated the place, and in May I moved out there with Debbie.

Running a bar on the Costa del Sol was a strange affair. Lots of people who've run pubs in the UK decide to move out to Spain to run a bar, thinking it's going to be all milk and honey, but it's a whole different ball game and, generally speaking, I really wouldn't recommend it. I was used to running a busy pub in the centre of

Nottingham, which is a big lively city. I was on my home turf, completely understood the language and the punters.

Fuengirola is no big city. It's not exactly small, though, and has a buzzing nightlife. Often featured in the *Costa del Crime* television series, it seems to attract lots of dubious characters who binge drink and get high on the easily available drugs. Spain is at the heart of drug running with cocaine and marijuana being smuggled across from Morocco and transported from there to several ports throughout Europe.

If someone was to ask me now whether it was a wise move to run a bar in Spain, I would categorically say, right here, right now, THINK VERY CAREFULLY and do your homework first. Check out the area and the kind of clientele you are likely to attract. From these basic observations, you will either sink or do very nicely.

Being an ex-pat brings more than its fair share of problems. For starters the calibre of people who move to the Costa del Sol is a tad dubious. I was told when I arrived that 90 per cent are wankers and to keep your eye on the other 10 per cent, and this is fantastic advice.

In Spain, where people can easily come and go, you must trust no one, and the more genuine they appear, the more likely they are to con you. You have to get to know someone over a long period before you can really allow them into your life.

Initially, I was very excited about my new venture. But I was soon reminded about the grass being greener. When life was becoming tough in Nottingham, and my finances were dwindling, I made the assumption that Spain would hold all the answers for me. Yes, I love Spain and, yes, I am still here, but you have to learn the rules and abide by them. That might sound harsh, but it's true. Once you've sifted out the rubbish, you will find the good guys and, once you've found them, you stick to them like glue.

One either loves or hates Fuengirola. I happen to quite like it with all its busy mayhem. The heart of the town is filled with street after street of shops selling anything and everything. Tall apartment blocks and hotels stretch for several miles along a coastline. In the height of summer, the narrow back streets and town are stiflingly hot and the traffic jams are horrendous. But the more time you spend in Fuengirola, the more you realise it has a strong personality of its own, and some quarters have managed to hold on to their Spanish identity, selling tapas and fine wines at reasonable prices.

As it's not far from Malaga airport, it was also handy for meeting my family and greeting friends who, thank God, visited me regularly in those early days when I was struggling to settle.

I called my bar Lloyd No.5. It was situated in a narrow lane near the well-known Fish Alley. I filled it with football memorabilia, and tried to make myself feel at home. I'd had such high hopes about this new start, but I knew from day one I'd made a huge mistake. It was dead – there were hardly any punters. But I just had to get on with it and hang on in there. The summer season was just around the corner; surely we'd be heaving soon?

I was wrapped up in trying to make the bar a success and attempting to keep my second marriage afloat, and I must admit I was still pretty down. If I'm honest, I didn't feel that Debbie and I were working together as a team – not in the way Sue and I had.

Second marriages can be harder to hold together than the first, especially if the first has lasted many years and produced children and grandchildren. For Debbie and I, there was also the little matter of a 17-year age gap. As much as I hated to admit it, Debbie's parents had had a point on that score.

So, this is how it worked. I ran the bar and Debbie worked there two nights a week. I employed a young girl to come in and give me an occasional break – those moments alone were a necessity for my mental health. I'd wander down the narrow lanes to the beach, and there I'd breathe in the sea air and watch the world go by.

I used to think that bloody bar attracted all the miserable bastards living on the Costa del Sol until I realised just how many miserable bastards live there! Nearly everyone was miserable, and that included me.

The tales of woe that were slurred over the bar wore me out. To be honest, I wasn't in the mood to listen to this shit day in and day out.

One day, this bloke sat there telling me all about the row he'd had with his wife, and I thought, 'Lloydie, why are you listening to this garbage?' I tell you, I could have kept that old sod there for three weeks had I decided to tell him *my* woes. Perhaps he'll pick up a copy of this book and recognise himself. I hope so. Mind you, there are so many unhappy people on the Costa del Sol who prop up bars and cry into their beer that hordes of them will wonder if I am talking about them.

The British holidaymakers would wander into Lloyd No.5 at Happy Hour for their 'buy one, get one free' drinks, all burned to a crisp, the men wearing sandals with socks and the women baring all this red flesh. Ugh! It was horrible.

I knew I had to get out – *mucho rapido*!

Fortunately, I was luckier than most bar owners who were desperately trying to sell up, because a buyer came forward quickly and I managed to get back what I'd paid for it. Not many people manage that in Spain. It's a tough game trying to make a decent living – and much harder than the gullible people who sell up their homes in the UK and move out there realise.

So we sold the bar and moved a little further up the road to an urbanisation called Calahonda, which is situated on the Costa del Sol, in between Fuengirola and Marbella.

We rented an apartment and then, with the equity from my lovely home in Nottingham, we bought a luxury apartment with beautiful sea views which we (or at least I) intended to be an investment.

I started to work in property sales, which to my surprise I really enjoyed. Debbie got a job working as a receptionist at a local radio station. Then she left again. She didn't like it. There's a surprise!

Soon after, she landed a job with a mortgage company and, hey, she liked it. Well, she liked the socialising part anyway. Her new boss loved to take his staff out after work, so three times a week Debbie would come home in the early hours worse for wear.

Needless to say, the cracks that were already in our marriage began to grow wider. I just wasn't prepared to put up with this behaviour. My earlier gut instincts about coming out to Spain on my own resurfaced, and misgivings about women having an agenda (that has nothing to do with love) swirled around in my head. I had come to realise that to 'want a man' was very different to 'needing a man'.

I had moved to sunny Spain, but my depression was forever surfacing. What was I doing with my life? What was I going to do about this farce of a marriage?

Debbie couldn't stand my bad moods, which, I must admit, were getting worse. My kids had nicknamed me 'Grump' many years before... now I *really was* Mr Grump. My wife hated me lounging around in my dressing gown, and the rows were constant. I had the attitude that, if the phone was going to ring, I could answer it just as well in that bloody old dressing gown. But she wasn't convinced.

But the phone rarely rang during that period, which was probably one of the reasons why I was so down all the time. There was the occasional real estate enquiry, but I had no enthusiasm for work, or anything else for that matter. I was burned out and lost.

My old mate John Robertson did call, so that was nice. But I guess you could say that I'd made myself a deep dugout and wasn't going to be easily moved. I knew nobody could pull me out of the mire but me.

I remember clearly the day I hit rock bottom. As usual, I had woken early. Anyone who has suffered from depression knows all about that darkest hour just before dawn – and I knew it well. With my dressing gown (which served as a security blanket) wrapped around me, I fell into the habit of making some coffee, lighting a cigarette and turning the television on to fill the silence.

Watching old black and white movies had become a way of escaping the demons that were invading my head, and there were plenty of entertaining John Wayne epics to enjoy – brilliant for taking you into a world of escapism.

This particular morning, the Western told the story of a little Indian boy. At the end of the movie, he fell down a cliff, crashed his head against a rock and died. The final scene showed a small gathering around the open grave at his burial. Just three people were present.

This scene had a huge impact, and I found myself weeping uncontrollably, while morbidly wondering about my own funeral. That was my watershed. That was the moment part of me died and another part came alive. After that I knew my life had to change – that *I* had to change.

I turned on my computer and 'Googled' myself. It was the weirdest feeling reading all about a man you could no longer identify with, but I made myself go back and re-experience everything. I had to find some sense of purpose again, as well as a new sense of 'self'.

I was sick and tired of being sick and tired. Somehow I had stepped outside this feeling of 'being alone'. Some people said I was a 'lost legend'. I didn't care about 'the legend' part of this label, but *I did* care about the 'lost' bit.

I knew I had to stop feeling sorry for myself and, in order to be able to do this, I started thinking about all those amazing men I had met throughout my career. What had happened to them? Where were they now?

I began to wonder about my life and my mortality. It was as if a light bulb had switched on and I could see clearer than ever before. I decided to start writing my diaries and found the more I wrote the more I learned about myself and I instantly knew it was time to document my life story.

CHAPTER 28:

THE FINAL CHAPTER

I USED TO be Larry Lloyd the footballer. I was the Bristol Rovers boy done good and then hero of the Kop. The lad who was going to be as good as Jackie Charlton, the one sent to Coventry who was dramatically rescued by Old Big 'Ed Clough and then became an international star and one of the Glory Boys at Nottingham Forest.

Most days, in general conversation, people ask, 'Do you remember him/her? Fuck me, yeah, wasn't he/she brilliant! Wonder whatever happened to them?'

Some heroes remain embraced by the media and given honours, their greatness celebrated, while others slip quietly into oblivion.

I've learned that, however much we want it to be, life is not about equality and fairness. It can be wonderful or it can be rotten. It can also be somewhere in the middle. Life as a professional footballer means life in the fast lane. When it's all over, you swerve into the slow lane or, if you are unlucky, on to the hard shoulder.

The trick is to somehow get into the middle lane and be content there – but it's not easy to find the middle lane of satisfaction, especially if you feel aggrieved, which is how I felt when I was unceremoniously kicked out of my jobs in Nottingham. I skidded on to the fucking hard shoulder then, I can tell you!

I have few regrets, but I've kind of always known I should have listened to Bob Paisley. He had promised me my first-team place back in due course and a pay rise – but hot-headed Lloydie thought he knew better. Fucking hell – what an idiot!

Never mind, the road less travelled and all that! What doesn't kill us makes us stronger. Christ, how I have to keep reminding myself of these words of wisdom.

My old team-mate Emlyn Hughes lived a quiet life after his playing career ended. He seemed to be happy and contented, giving occasional after-dinner speeches and enjoying his charity and media work. We lost Emlyn too young from a brain tumour – he was just 57. Makes you feel grateful you still have life, even though you *do* feel a bit lost!

I have had a passion for our great national game since I was a young boy in the 1950s. Today we have magnificent stadiums both in Britain and around the world. There is underground heating and the grass is lush and perfect. But in contrast we slogged our guts out on pitches that reflected the harsh British weather, often when the ground was rock hard with very little grass to protect our skin and bones. Other times, when pitches were waterlogged, with mud oozing, we got soaked.

It used to be a family affair – granddads, dads, uncles, brothers, sons and, of course, mates. It was a man's game then, and we were men who earned our crust the hard way. Nowadays, if the extended family wants to go to a top soccer match, they have to take out a bloody mortgage – and that would exclude a half-time hot-dog and overpriced programme!

That said, football is going nowhere. It is here to stay.

I have been blessed to live so much of my life in the world of football, mixing with so many great characters who have helped to mould Larry Lloyd into the wise old bugger I have become. I am also well aware there are plenty of men who would give their right arm to experience the life I've had.

It doesn't take much thinking to muster up the incredible throbbing atmosphere, and the maelstrom of noise coming from the Kop at Anfield as they sang 'You'll Never Walk Alone', or the Trent End at Nottingham as we ran out of the tunnel to the tune of 'Robin Hood… Robin Hood…', the stands a wall of red.

I was respected, feared and admired by strikers from other teams. I loved it, and I'm proud of it. I was a hard bastard, a brick wall and a hot-headed idiot at times. That was me – that was Larry Lloyd.

I was asked recently whether I like living in Spain or if I would like to move back to Nottingham. That's a difficult question. I love living by the sea, and adore the sunshine, even though it gets a bit much during the summer months. But there is no doubt in my mind that life back in Nottingham holds an attraction as well. I guess I'm lucky to be able to call both places 'home'.

Nowadays I am part of a fabulous company that deals with property in the holiday industry. The owners, Paul Duff and Graham Manuel, are terrific guys. I think if Paul had been involved in football he would have made a great manager – his motivational skills are excellent. As for Graham, well, would you believe it! He's a big Nottingham Forest fan so, needless to say, we always have plenty to chat about. He thinks nothing of flying to Nottingham on a Friday night to watch the team on a Saturday, before flying back to his home on the Costa.

Paul, Graham and their two managers, Kevin Newbound and Andy Scrawley have created a nice little niche for me in their PR department. This time there is no David Platt to contend with, which makes me very happy. These guys fall into the 'good guys' category, the decent characters you eventually find after you've stumbled through the dangerous 'Costa del Despair' minefield and survived.

I still have just two of the vices that Peter Taylor required of his players – smoking and drinking – and I have no intention of giving them up. I've always been a big colossus of a man, but now the soft centre that was hidden deep inside is very much on the surface and if you don't bloody like it you know what you can do!

People may only recognise me as an ex-footballer who used to go by the name of Larry Lloyd. But, if you want to know who I am, I'm Larry Lloyd, the most underrated player of his time. You can call me fat bastard too if you like – both are pretty fitting.

With my second marriage now over, I find solace living by the calming sea and surrounded by the Andalucian Mountains. I like to sit in my favourite bar on a rocky cliff, with a glass of white wine in my hand and a plate of Spanish tapas on the table in front of me. Nowadays, my blue eyes peer out at the world from underneath white eyebrows, and I see more clearly than I did in my hot-headed youth.

I love to gaze across the rocks and watch the ocean. I have always had a fascination with water. The unpredictability of the tides and the power of the sea reflect my personality in many ways, so I feel connected to the elements.

Writing this book has been quite some journey. Now, as I wrap it up, I hope this will be a replacement gift for Yolanda, Damian and my granddaughter Georgia. A kind of apology for selling my medals that should have rightly been theirs when old 'Pop' pegs it.

THE FINAL CHAPTER

Yolanda told me the other day that, when Georgia heard I was writing my memoirs, she Googled me! My daughter told me that *her* daughter was just as proud of old 'Pop' as *she* had been as a child, and that brought a tear to my eye, I can tell you.

I cry easily, and throughout this journey, as I've spoken about my father and other emotional memories, I have cried an ocean. That's just how I am. But I am a great believer in shedding tears.

So, I sit here now, with memories of the Bristol Rovers boys, Shankly's gravelly voice echoing in my head, and Sir Alf's posh voice incongruently saying, 'Fuck!' when he witnessed the hilarious sight of Frank 'Elvis' Worthington swaggering towards him in his cowboy hat and boots. I can see the terror etched on Kevin Keegan's face as Kenny Burns took his teeth out in the tunnel at the Bernabeu, and then Robbo's right foot shooting that cracking goal in the back of the net to win us the European Cup.

I smile a lot too, so there's a balance going on to counteract the tears. I still growl from time to time but those who love me forgive me… eventually.

My eyes scan the Mediterranean now and, as I peer further out into the sparkling sea with crazy white horses rearing up, I think about the crazy horse Emlyn Hughes, the boy who nicked Tommy Smith's breakfast and died too young.

I recall the wonderful memories of when Yolanda and Damian came into the world, and then, much later, when Georgia was born.

Then I drift into thinking about my one and only real hero – my dad. The first image I visualise is of me sitting on the end of his bed as a teenager sharing my problems and listening to his words of wisdom. Then I remember him holding baby Yolanda, before shutting his eyes and drifting peacefully away.

So I take a mouthful of a delicious meaty prawn and wash it down with the wine, before ordering some coffee and Spanish brandy. Ah! Life can be sweet.

As I sip the hot tipple, one of my favourite tunes of the Motown era begins to play. They play great music in this little bar.

The same tape of golden oldies play over and over again, but I don't mind. I'm a golden oldie myself. 'Behind a Painted Smile' is followed by 'Tears of a Clown'. The only song not playing, which would make this moment perfect, is 'Concrete and Clay' by Unit 4+2, but, then, life might be sweet but it's far from perfect. Nothing's perfect – not even Cloughie – although, if he could disagree from his grave, he would.

Finally I think about my favourite movie, the classic starring James Stewart. It's called *It's a Wonderful Life.*